AND IT'S A BEAUTIFUL DAY

A FARGO COMPANION

NIGE TASSELL

POLARIS
PUBLISHING

First published in 2021 by

POLARIS PUBLISHING LTD
c/o Aberdein Considine
2nd Floor, Elder House
Multrees Walk
Edinburgh
EH1 3DX

www.polarispublishing.com

Distributed by
BIRLINN LIMITED

To the darn tootin' KP

CONTENTS

INTRODUCTION

We start a couple of blocks from the Mississippi River.

But this isn't the Mississippi as it makes its glacial passage from near its source in upcountry Minnesota. Nor is this the section of the great river where it bisects, and then curls around, Minneapolis. You might expect a book on *Fargo* to start in either place. And justifiably so. Those are the film's killing fields, after all.

Instead, we're 1,700-odd miles downriver from Minneapolis. We're in New Orleans, close to the point at which the defrosted waters of the northern lakes end their journey in the salty Gulf of Mexico. New Orleans and Minneapolis might share a river, and a time zone, but it's another country down here, far closer in both distance and meteorology to the Caribbean than to the frozen tundra of the north. Just count the palm trees.

It's 1996 – late morning on the second Friday of March, to be exact – and you find us standing in line to get into a New Orleans picture house, the Canal Place Cinema. We (me and girlfriend/future wife Jane) have been in the city for little more than a few hours. We got in late last night. But rather than fully throw ourselves into the bountiful cultural riches that New Orleans has to offer, we're starting the day – the whole two-week trip, in fact – by skipping out of the sunshine to sit in a darkened movie theatre and watch a soot-black thriller with a hefty body count. There will be blood.

The subject of murder had already been raised that morning, when the Southern hospitality of our B&B host extended to unfolding a tourist map of the city across our breakfast table. She reached for a pen and drew circles around entire neighbourhoods. Perhaps she was recommending we take a gentle stroll through these particular areas. Maybe she thought them as delightful as the magnolia-scented streets of her own Garden District. She wasn't and she didn't. 'Do NOT go into these areas,' she instructed, shooting us the fiercest of looks. 'You WILL be killed.' She meant it. There would be blood.

Standing in that cinema line, a clanking streetcar ride later, our fellow film-goers didn't look like the bloodlust kind. We were almost exclusively bookish types, bespectacled specimens with a low Vitamin D intake who had decided to venture out into the dazzling sunlight of downtown New Orleans for a very special reason that Friday morning. For these followers of cinema, 8 March 1996 was a red-letter day: the occasion of the first showing, on the first morning of release, of the new film from Joel and Ethan Coen.

As *Fargo*'s opening credits rolled, the brethren sat in hushed reverence. A quiet murmur greeted the name of Frances McDormand – the star of the brothers' first film, 1984's *Blood Simple*, as well as being the wife of the elder Coen. The whispered approval was a little quieter for William H. Macy, at that point midway through his tenure as chief surgeon Dr Morgenstern on *ER*. And you could sense everyone was nodding in the dark when the name of Coen brothers veteran Steve Buscemi appeared on screen. Buscemi was always great value.

We would be in safe hands.

But there was also a wisp of nervousness in the air. After a run of much-loved offerings – *Miller's Crossing* and *Barton Fink* in particular – the Coens' previous film, *The Hudsucker Proxy*, had been a stylised affair which had satisfied neither critics nor fans. And it certainly hadn't satisfied the bean counters of PolyGram and Warner Bros. The rumour was that its box-office take had recovered barely a tenth of its production budget. What we'd read about *Fargo* in advance – and, obviously, we had tried to keep that to a minimum so that the on-screen events could unfold without presupposition – was that it was a return to film noir for the siblings, a retreading of the territory of that debut, *Blood Simple*. The poster in the cinema lobby confirmed this: a reproduction of a cross-stitch embroidery featuring a car on its roof and a corpse leaking blood onto virgin white snow. Where *The Hudsucker Proxy* had been polished to a shine, *Fargo* would be gritty and raw. Necessity dictated it would need to be low-budget too.

We needn't have worried. Ninety-four minutes later, we blindly stumbled back outside into the scorch of lunchtime New Orleans, fully satiated by what we'd just seen – a brilliantly taut thriller endowed with a near-perfect confluence of plot, script and performance. And several laughs too. We'd just been told a timeless morality tale, one that, having been given a 1987 date stamp on this occasion, took the form of a modern-day Western (or Midwestern?). A pregnant police chief occupied the John Wayne role, rounding up the outlaws aboard her not-so-trusty steed – an unreliable Brainerd Police Department prowler.

The film critic from the local paper, the *Times-Picayune*, may have been among us. If so, he wouldn't have looked as relieved and thrilled as us. The best adjectives he would later use in his review were curious ones: 'gothic' and 'loony'. *Barton Fink* was gothic, while their second film, *Raising Arizona*, could be classed as loony. Neither adjective matched *Fargo*. This critic's overall summation was that it was a 'solid effort'. He was wrong again. *Fargo* was, in my immediate opinion, a masterwork, and undeniably the pinnacle of the brothers' achievements thus far.

Quite often, instant evaluations diminish over the years as the passing of time recalibrates taste and expectation. Contexts change and opinions shift. New benchmarks are set. But over the quarter-century since that March morning, my appreciation, my outright enjoyment, of *Fargo* has faded not a shade. The *Times-Picayune* reviewer may have hedged his bets and fudged his words, but my initial verdict remains secured to the mast I nailed it to back in 1996. No revisionist appraisal has been necessary over the years. I got it right first time. *Fargo* remains, in my eyes, untouchable. It might be set in the flatlands of Minnesota, but it's a film that occupies the highest of altitudes. Nothing else can cast a shadow upon it.

The critic Clive James once used a motor-racing analogy when talking of Aaron Sorkin's *The West Wing*. To James, the seven-series political drama was the high-water mark of Sorkin's creativity, a time at which he was 'racing on the crown of the asphalt'. With his later creations, *Studio 60 on the Sunset Strip* and *The Newsroom*, Sorkin subsequently 'spent a lot of time on the grass', having misjudged the track ahead of him. This is how I feel about *Fargo*. Certain Coen movies haven't always smoothly steered the tightest of racing lines (see here the cold and distant *The Man Who Wasn't There*, for example). But *Fargo* stays firmly on the asphalt from start to finish, its tyres barely an inch out of place. And it started a run of victories for the Coens. Their next two films, *The Big Lebowski* and *O Brother, Where Art Thou?*, never went near the grass either.

Fargo's script was witty and sharp, its characters well-drawn, and the story taut. Not an ounce of fat was left on it. And, of course, such is the Coens' legendary meticulousness, barely a single bullet-hole could be found in the plot either. Had the brothers opted for a life of crime rather than a life of creating Oscar-winning movies, there would be few criminal masterminds to rival them when it came to drawing up a plan – for a heist, a kidnapping, a murder – as watertight as one from their twin forensic minds. Every eventuality would have been chewed over and measured by the pair, the tiniest detail checked, double-checked, triple-checked. They are masters of anticipating, and answering, the 'But what if . . . ?'

Perhaps my ardour for *Fargo* was so absolute even before the closing credits had disappeared, and has remained so over the decades, because there was a strong tang of familiarity about it. For me, *Fargo* had a head-start on the other American crime movies of the mid-1990s, a reason for me to cherish and defend it for ever.

Between the film's fictional setting of 1987 and its release nine years later, I lived in Minnesota – in Minneapolis, to be exact, just two blocks from the Mississippi. I knew the state's sub-zero months, its heavy snowfall, its treacherous ice-capped sidewalks, its lost highways, its flat horizons, its family restaurants, its unfailing politeness, its reliance on maximum-tog winter-wear.

Knowing the landscape meant the film spoke to me in more intimate tones than those of other crime movies – the Los Angeles of *Reservoir Dogs*, *Pulp Fiction* and *The Usual Suspects*, or the Detroit of *True Romance*, or the, um, Denver of *Things to Do in Denver When You're Dead* . . . I recognised the Minnesota-specific reference points that would be throwaway mentions to most film-goers, but which the punctilious Coens added to the script in anything but throwaway fashion. I regularly watched the Gophers, the catch-all name of the University of Minnesota's various sports teams so beloved of Wade Gustafson. I knew the lakeside suburb of Wayzata where Jerry Lundegaard planned to put his fortune-making parking lots. And I was a regular at my local branch of Embers, the Minnesota chain of all-night diners where Jerry, Wade and Stan Grossman discuss the tactics they'll adopt with the kidnappers.

And I stood up for the film not just because I used to live there, but because – other than *Purple Rain* and *Graffiti Bridge* – films didn't tend to be set in Minnesota. (The similarly snowbound *A Simple Plan*, released two years later and directed by Coen collaborator Sam Raimi, shared *Fargo*'s themes of greed, murder and a big stash of cash, but never came close to matching the majesty of its forerunner.)

Until *Fargo*, American crime films tended to play out before a backdrop of New York City, Las Vegas or southern California. But bad deeds could be – and were being – committed across that big chunk of land in between. It wasn't a haven of virtue and goodness; it turned out there were schemes and evil dreams in the heads of the cutesy folks of Middle America. As one of the film's taglines had it, 'a lot can happen in the middle of nowhere'. Ever the champion of the underdog, I was showing perverse pride at Hollywood finally showing the aptitude of Minnesotan residents (albeit *fictional* ones) for doing Very Bad Things. Weird, no?

I've watched *Fargo* far more times than I've watched any other film. Way, way more. Some people treat *The Godfather* this way, or perhaps *Star Wars*. I know every facial expression, every line down to the last 'Yah'. And I still unconsciously quote from it. I might find myself responding to a social media comment I approve of with 'You're darn tootin''. Or, in admonishing one of my kids for a minor infraction, I'll lay down the law with 'I'm not gonna debate you, [insert name of misbehaving offspring here]'.

But just as it's been a while since I've been back to Minnesota, it's also been a while since I've been back to *Fargo*. A friend of mine devoted her teen years to an evangelical allegiance to the music and the members of Queen. Obsessed, she was. But then, in adulthood, she abruptly got rid of all her Queen records. It wasn't simply that she'd put away such childish things. Instead, she reasoned that every last bassline, every last guitar riff, every last Freddie Mercury wail was stored in her head and would be for eternity. Records just took up space and, if she wanted to hear a particular song, the jukebox in her brain would simply spring into action.

Using that logic, do I really need to watch *Fargo* ever again? I know every twist and every turn of those ninety-four minutes, every lesson it imparts, every last 'You betcha'. What can I learn from it, what can I learn of it, that I don't already know?

Maybe there are some secrets still buried in the snow. Let's head back north one more time to find out – to step in its footprints, visit its diners, smell its fresh blood.

But don't forget to wrap up warm though, yah?

ONE

THE TRUTH IS OUT THERE

'There are no whole truths,' the British mathematician turned American philosopher Alfred North Whitehead once declared. 'All truths are half-truths. It is trying to treat them as whole truths that plays the devil.'

In the double-barrelled imaginations of the Coen brothers, truths even being half-truths is rather a generous appraisal.

For serial watchers of *Fargo*, there are forty-three words as familiar as the Pledge of Allegiance faithfully recited by American schoolchildren every morning. Forty-three words scorched indelibly on the front of their brain. They could repeat them in their sleep. Cue the opening titles.

THIS IS A TRUE STORY.

The events depicted in this film took place in Minnesota in 1987.

At the request of the survivors, the names have been changed.

Out of respect for the dead, the rest has been told exactly as it occurred.

Throughout the press campaign ahead of the film's release in March 1996, the Coens maintained that each and every fold and crease of *Fargo*'s plot, every twist and every turn, was based in reality, based on events that had transpired as gruesomely as they retold them. Like a politician in denial about a sexual indiscretion, both individually and collectively the brothers were steadfast in their defence, pushing an untruth about a truth that was itself an untruth.

They were gobsmackingly brazen about it. 'Everything we have done before has been entirely fictional,' declared Joel in the film's official production notes. '*Fargo*, on the other hand, was a conscious effort to explore the spectrum of a series of non-fictional events.'

This brazenness continued when the Coens went eyeball-to-eyeball with journalists for interviews prior to the release. They managed to suppress any sniggers. They didn't guiltily shift in their chairs. They held the interviewer's gaze. It was a united front of falsehood.

'How close was the script to the actual event?' asked the legendary film critic Peter Biskind.

'Pretty close,' deadpanned Ethan.

'We wanted to do something that was unlike the movies we had done in the past,' Joel expanded, 'which were all sort of self-consciously artificial. We wanted to try something based on a real story.'

Another interview, another journalist, another question concerning the veracity of the tale. How had they found out about the original case and why hadn't it received much attention at the time?

'It's astonishing how things of that nature receive so little publicity,' bluffed Ethan playfully. 'We heard about it through a friend who lived near to where the drama took place in Minnesota.'

No such case. No such friend.

But, at this point, the media was unaware of this. Editors despatched their best reporters to seek out the original story, amazed that this complex web of deception, with a trail of dead that was both bloody and high (bloody high, in fact), had gone largely unreported in the nine years since it happened.

Of course, after hours spent trawling through dusty newspaper archives or putting calls in to law-enforcement agencies in upcountry Minnesota, they found nothing that tallied with the Coens' tall tale.

'The *New York Post* found out it wasn't based on any case studies and wasn't true at all,' William H. Macy later told an audience at the Florida Film Festival. Joel and Ethan, reeling with faux horror, responded in quintessential Coen fashion: 'We're shocked something like this could have happened. An internal investigation is going on. Three people from our staff have been let go. We want to assure the public that they can expect quality entertainment from us in the future.'

With their duty to undertake all those interviews having been met, queues having formed nicely at cinemas, and tills a-ringing, the Coens began to come clean. Confession time.

In his introduction to Faber's publication of the film's screenplay, Ethan used the example of tales that his grandmother used to tell in order to muse on the nature of true stories, on how they bend and reshape themselves over multiple tellings. They get embellished with half-truths and fabrications. The boring bits get dropped. They become finely honed pieces of unreliable memoir, often only palely resembling the original events. And, of course, the stories of grandparents always find a believing audience among the wide-eyed offspring of their own offspring.

The Coen brothers' fans would regard the pronouncements of their heroes with the same credulity that grandchildren offer. If they said it were so, if they said it were true, why should they doubt it?

After a lengthy ramble of one of Grandma's possibly tall tales (indeed, was his story about his grandmother's possibly tall tales a possible tall tale itself?), Ethan devoted just one short paragraph of the introduction to *Fargo* itself. His final sentence was a clear admission: 'It aims to be both homey and exotic, and pretends to be true.'

No guilt was felt by the Coens, though. This wasn't a deception of Jerry Lundegaard proportions. If a film-maker can come up with a fictional story, then it follows, with perfect logic, that a 'true story' notice at the start – but still within the parameters of the film itself – could be fictional too. As Ethan later explained, 'You don't have to have a true story to make a "true story" movie.'

The notice wasn't included simply for the purposes of the Coens to make some mischief at the expense of those sitting out in the stalls. There was method behind it. 'If they're told upfront that it's true,' Joel reasoned, 'the audience gives you permission to do things that they might not if they're essentially coming in expecting to watch a fictive thriller.' Furthermore, by claiming the whole sordid episode to be true, the drabness, the ordinariness of its setting could be justified.

Ethan hinted that the original intention might have been to find a suitably bloodstained real-life case deserving of being transferred to the big screen. But they drew a blank. 'Not being acquainted with any true crimes that seemed sufficiently compelling, we made up our own "true crime" story.'

Years later – and we're talking twenty years later – in an interview with the *Huffington Post*, Joel put more meat on the bones of the cases that did at least partly inspire the writing of *Fargo*. 'There are actually two little elements in the story that were based on actual incidents. One of them is the fact that there was a guy – I believe, in the '60s or '70s – who was gumming up serial numbers for cars and defrauding the General Motors Finance Corporation. There was no kidnapping. There was no murder.

'The other thing based on something real: there was a murder in Connecticut, where a man killed his wife and disposed of the body – put her into a wood chipper. But, beyond that, the story is made up.'

That he was still having to answer to the issue of truth a full two decades after the film's release suggests the Coens were a little more adroit at playing Alfred North Whitehead's devil than they might have thought.

TWO

GOD'S ICEBOX

Fargo's opening titles set the film's temperature.

The screen is a pale blue. There's nothing yet to define it, to give it context and meaning. It could be the endless pale blue of a Californian sky; perhaps a 747 is just about to bisect it on its descent into LAX.

Underneath the delicately plucked and strummed harp that's picking out a mournful folk tune, a sound can be heard. It's a scorching sound, but it's also a kind of hum. It could be that 747. Or a whistling wind. Or, as it actually is, an approaching vehicle.

A fiddle takes over the melody and the dark outline of a bird is partly visible in the distance, dipping and bobbing. A line of telegraph poles starts to appear, and then the distant twin headlights of an oncoming car. This is definitely not the endless pale blue of a Californian sky. This is the blue of cold, the blue murk of midwinter rural

Minnesota, the point of the year when land and sky merge, indistinguishable from each other, with no visible horizon to keep them apart.

It's cold out there. Proper cold. Coldness that chills the bones and slows the bloodstream. Coldness that can be deadly. This opening shot is a suggestion to do up an extra button because this will be the core temperature for the next hour and a half.

But what else would you expect from a film set in Minnesota? Aside from Alaska – part of which, of course, falls within the Arctic Circle – it's the most northerly state in the union. During January and February, it's not untypical for temperatures in the northern half to fall as low as minus thirty degrees Fahrenheit. The extreme winter weather defines the place in many American eyes. It's a large part of its identity. And, thanks to *Fargo*'s international success, it's what non-Americans know most about Minnesota too. As the *New Yorker*'s review of the film noted, the state 'appears to be auditioning for a permanent role as God's icebox'.

Minnesota's location – between North Dakota and Wisconsin, nudging up against the Canadian border – doesn't help its susceptibility to the elements. Its flatlands, much of which have been deforested across the centuries to be turned into pasture and cereal fields, encourage high winds that bring the chill down from Canada. There are few contours, few natural barriers, to get in the way of these winds. They're uncontested. There's no escape from their power, or from the heavy snows they carry with them.

The cityscape of the Twin Cities of Minneapolis-Saint Paul doesn't escape the weather either, although the metropolitan area has legislated for it over the years. Many of the buildings in downtown Minneapolis are linked by the extensive Skyway System – a nine-and-a-half-mile network of indoor pedestrian bridges that connect skyscraper to skyscraper. These offer warm passage, two levels up, right across the downtown area between offices, banks, department stores and food courts. Indeed, it's possible for an office worker to commute from their suburban garage to their high-rise desk and back – and also head off at lunchtime to dine, shop or do their banking – without having to take a single breath of freezing Minnesota air. The city is justifiably proud of this innovative system. One of its great musical exports, The Replacements, even eulogised it in their imaginatively titled song 'Skyway'.

Minneapolitans have adapted and evolved to live full lives in this intemperate climate, to ensure that winter isn't simply a period of hibernation. The Twin Cities' sandy outdoor volleyball courts of summer are deliberately flooded when the mercury starts to plummet. Within a couple of days, nature has converted them into makeshift ice rinks for the playing of broomball – a derivation of ice hockey, but instead played with a broom and a small ball, with players wearing rubber-soled shoes and no protective gear.

Minnesota's many lakes – 10,000 according to the slogan on the state's licence plates, although the actual total is a few thousand higher – also enjoy dual use. In high summer, the lakes become a playground for all manner of water sports. In winter, skidoos replace jet skis, roaring along on ice that can be as much as fifteen inches thick. Ice fishing is also a popular pastime, whereby a hole is drilled into the ice and a line dropped into the dark, chilly depths. Sometimes the fisher-folk are exposed to the elements; more prepared types go about their business from the comparative luxury of a portable ice shack. And wherever you drive in deep midwinter, be sure to have tyre chains in your car's trunk in case of sudden, otherwise incapacitating snowfall.

It's unclear whether the car in *Fargo*'s opening titles has tyre chains on. As the fiddle fades, the vehicle disappears from view. Then, as the timpani pounds and the orchestra swells, it re-emerges, riding a rise in the road. At this point, the score – written by Coen brothers regular Carter Burwell – sounds too overblown, too majestic. The triumphal weight of the orchestration sounds more appropriate to a Civil War epic, the accompaniment to a general vanquishing his army's foe. It certainly sounds excessive when soaring over an extended shot of a nondescript car pulling another car on a trailer along a nondescript highway. What is there to be so triumphant about?

Subsequent viewings will confirm that the purpose of the booming score at this early point is to hint at the heaviness yet to come. This is a warning.

THREE

'I'M NOT GONNA DEBATE YOU, JERRY . . .'

The trailer-pulling car makes its way along the slushy streets of Fargo, North Dakota, before turning into the parking lot of a neighbourhood bar, the King of Clubs. The first shots of the bar's interior confirm that this is a joint that doesn't come close to living up to its name. It's an anonymous, unremarkable place. Country music plays on the jukebox, while the obligatory game of pool is in progress. Both are cinematic shorthand for a blue-collar or redneck bar. Cue another well-turned trope: the outsider making his entry into this alien environment.

But that's where the Coens take a different tack to lesser film-makers. As the outsider stomps the snow off his boots at the door, the jukebox doesn't go silent, nor does the pool game come to a sudden halt. This is no biker bar ready to explode into a tangle of violence meted out with pool cues. The woman behind the bar wears a homely Scandinavian sweater, while the clientele, in their flannel shirts and overalls, are largely on the dark side of sixty. They have no desire for any kind of rumpus. They don't even notice the outsider, presumably the driver who pulled into the parking lot a few moments before, as he makes his way towards the far end of the bar, serenaded by the strains of Merle Haggard's 'Big City'. (The sharp of ear will notice how the song's lyrics refer to the elusive dream of financial independence, a theme that underpins the film.)

The outsider – his shirt and tie visible under a thickly padded jacket – has no difficulty identifying who he's supposed to be meeting up with: the two men, notably younger than the rest of the clientele, sitting alongside each other in a booth, with half a dozen beer bottles on the table. One of them is dozing, a stubbled, thick-set man with swept-back peroxide hair and a cigarette hanging from his mouth. The other – from this first impression, at least – is a comparative sophisticate in a pale lemon roll-neck. We will come to discover, of course, that first impressions can deceive.

This is the first time that these three individuals have met, so, handily for viewers, introductions are made. The outsider reveals himself to be Jerry Lundegaard, while the roll-necked one does the talking for the pair: 'I'm Carl Showalter and this is my associate Gaear Grimsrud.' But we can see that – from the rough demeanour of Grimsrud alone, and despite use of the phrase 'my associate' – this isn't going to be a meeting about legitimate business concerns. Those kinds of meetings aren't generally held to a soundtrack of outlaw country music and clinking Miller Lite bottles.

The balance of power within the triumvirate is quickly revealed. Showalter takes charge immediately, clearly a seasoned campaigner when it comes to criminal assignations in the far corners of low-lit dives like this. Wide-eyed Jerry is out of his depth immediately, lacking the chops to go toe-to-toe. Ground is instantly conceded, and apologies offered. 'I'm sure sorry,' he splutters when Showalter informs him he's an hour late. 'It was a mix-up, I guess.' He's a submissive puppy, rolling over for the bigger dogs to dominate and bully. He'll never be their equal. This is a man – a deeply nervous man – losing his criminal cherry. And he is far from a master of the necessary foreplay.

Showalter – well, Steve Buscemi at least – has been here before: sitting at a table in a film's opening tableau, taking on refreshment ahead of a job. But in *Reservoir Dogs*, as the disagreeable Mr Pink, he was in the company of similarly besuited wise guys, shooting the breeze over breakfast in a competitive manner about insignificant subjects, such as the true meanings of various Madonna songs. From the evidence offered so far, Showalter and Mr Pink appear to be characters cut from the same cloth. Both are mildly abrasive. And both look a hell of a lot like Steve Buscemi.

Certainly, the refusal of Mr Pink to throw in a single dollar for the waitress's tip (because she's only refilled his cup three times, and he likes it done twice as often) has echoes in a scene in *Fargo* where Showalter questions the legitimacy of being charged four dollars by the attendant at the airport parking lot when he was only there for as long as it took to unscrew and steal the licence plates from another car. In these respective scenes, both Showalter and Mr Pink take occupation of (a somewhat flawed) moral high ground, putting misplaced principles ahead of trivial amounts of money. 'These are the limits of your life, man,' Showalter snarls, reaching for his wallet. 'Ruler of your little fucking gate here. Here, here's your four dollars, you pathetic piece of shit.'

Let's go further. There's certainly some sport to be had in positing that Showalter is actually the real identity of Mr Pink, that they are one and the same. It's unclear at the end of Tarantino's movie whether Mr Pink – the only one of the hoodlums not to be mortally wounded in the blizzard of post-heist double- and triple-crossing – gets arrested or manages to escape with the diamonds. Either way, whether now freshly sprung from jail or having gone into immediate hiding after his getaway, it's fun to believe that Mr Pink trimmed that goatee down to a moustache and swapped Los Angeles for the anonymity of the Midwest. In this new life, however – as per the theme of Merle Haggard's song – he didn't relinquish his desire for an existence where easy money can be made without the drudgery of the nine-to-five. His is still a life of crime.

Tarantino shot *Reservoir Dogs'* opening scene with arch coolness and deliberate obliqueness. Little information is forthcoming about the men's identities (throughout, we will only know each one of them, except Joe the boss and his son Eddie, by their designated, colour-themed pseudonyms), nor the purpose for which they've all gathered. The Coens take an approach that's way more functional and user-friendly. After Jerry Lundegaard's apologies and nervous conversation that further confirms his discomfort in the position he's found himself in ('I got every confidence here in you fellas'), Showalter's confusion over the logic of Jerry's plan handily allows for a summation of what will unfold over the next few days in these characters' lives – and in the next hour and a half of ours. Showalter and Grimsrud will kidnap Jerry's wife, his rich father-in-law will pay the $80,000 ransom, and Jerry will give them $40,000 (plus the car), while trousering the rest for his own personal needs.

But while the essence of the plan – and therefore the film's plot – is neatly distilled at such an early stage, we've not been spoon-fed everything. In this opening scene, Jerry's motivation for hatching the conspiracy remains obscure. Those personal needs go undisclosed – 'I'm not gonna go inta, inta – see, I just need the money.' Not everything is revealed early doors. And neither will it necessarily be by the time the closing credits roll. (For now too, Jerry's intention to double-cross the kidnappers – by demanding a $1m ransom from his father-in-law but keeping the remaining

$960,000 for himself – remains a secret. It's only on further, hindsight-endowed viewings of this opening scene that we might trawl over the details and realise that $40,000 is far too trifling a sum to put close family members into such turmoil for, even in 1987 money.)

Grimsrud is silent for almost the entirety of this scene, setting the template – those future bursts of vicious violence aside – for the rest of the film. It's only when Jerry explains that the car is the down-payment and that the kidnappers' share of the proceeds will come later, after the ransom's been paid, that we see the big Swede react. Until now, he's maintained the same slouched position, with only his half-open eyes telling us he's awake. Now, having heard a possible breach of what had previously been agreed, he sits up and leans intimidatingly over the table towards Jerry, his nostrils expelling plumes of cigarette smoke. 'It's not a whole pay-in-advance deal,' Jerry whimpers, as if he were negotiating with one of his car-buying customers.

Showalter's words – and Grimsrud's to-the-bone stare – try to grind him down. But the former is half-hearted in his protestations. He knows this is no equal battle of wills. Before him, he sees a weak man who can be dominated, never suspecting for a moment that this dope possesses the wit, or the nerve, to double-cross the pair. 'I'm not gonna debate you, Jerry,' he announces. 'I'm not gonna sit here and debate.' The car – the brand-new burnt umber Ciera sitting outside on the trailer – is accepted as down-payment.

This opening scene is the only scene of the entire film set in the town that gives the movie its name, a town just over the border from Minnesota. It's one of just two scenes that take place in North Dakota. All the bloodied, brutal, double-crossing action occurs back across the state line. But this scene more than earns its keep. It's imparted plenty already, allowing us to form swift but sturdy opinions about each of the three characters. Fewer than four minutes in, we know that Jerry Lundegaard is a desperate man but, as one who's willing to use his wife as an unwitting pawn in a dangerous plan, he's already lost our sympathy. Perhaps we shouldn't refer to him as Jerry. First names are reserved for heroes, after all.

And the chances are that we won't be cheering on Showalter or Grimsrud any time soon either.

FOUR

HOME TURF

If it's a sunny day in Minneapolis, a wander along the sidewalks and grass verges of Flag Avenue South – a tree-lined residential street in the suburb of St Louis Park – is by no means a disagreeable way to pass some time.

On its southern stretch, the street runs alongside the manicured greens and well-tended fairways of Minneapolis Golf Club. At its northern end, it curls around the wilder lands of Westwood Hills Nature Center, a large area of woods, marshland and restored prairie that sits just behind the houses. It's at this end of the street that you'll find number 1425. Nothing makes it stand out from any of the other homes on Flag Avenue South. It's just another three-bedroomed, detached property – not small but certainly not any kind of showy mansion – set at the top of a sloping lawn, with a double garage underneath. All the houses nearby have been built to the same template. You can't tell one from another.

Number 1425 has a basketball hoop set up on the driveway, and an ice hockey goal – complete with cut-out goaltender – in front of the garage door. A sports-mad teen or two clearly lives here. The boys who called this house their home back in the 1960s and early '70s almost certainly didn't have such a set-up on the driveway. They weren't jocks. They weren't the outdoor types very much at all; while Westwood Hills, just over the fence of their backyard, invited storybook Huckleberry Finn-esque childhood adventures, the two brothers declined the offer.

Instead, the siblings – let's call them Joel and Ethan Coen, for that's who they are – preferred to stay indoors, certainly during the big chill of those extended Minnesotan winters. Inside number 1425, they would draw the curtains, switch on the television and slump down onto sofas. Here they would indulge and develop their love of movies: absorbing styles, genres and influences, while teaching themselves the principles of cinematography, the pattern of plot, the nuance of dialogue. They soaked it up – through the pores and into the bloodstream. Weekends and school holidays were lost to cinema as they pinballed their way back and forth across big-screen history. Some favourites rose to the surface: *The Big Sleep*, *The Long Goodbye*, *Dr. Strangelove*, *The Outlaw Josey Wales*, *Chinatown*, even *The Bad News Bears* . . .

The brothers would emerge, dazzled and blinking, once the sunshine had returned and the snows had thawed. They would spend summers mowing their neighbours' lawns to raise the money to pay for their first film camera, a Vivitar Super 8 bought with cash in a downtown Minneapolis store. Returning to the 'burbs, the avenues of St Louis Park would be the backdrop for their first cinematic attempts.

(The Coens didn't leave the place back there, back in their adolescence. They returned to the St Louis Park of their youth – specifically 1967 – to set 2009's *A Serious Man* there. The address of the film's lead character, a Jewish physics professor, is 1425 Flag Avenue South. The Coens' father was a Jewish economics professor – see the subtle difference? – who, of course, lived at number 1425 at that time. The pair are clearly advocates of the 'use everything' advice that seasoned writers are known to suggest to ears-open wannabes.)

There's never been a plaque attached to the side of the house declaring its importance to American film history.

And there's no tourist bus shuttling back and forth between here and that other monument to world-leading Minneapolitan culture, Prince's Paisley Park studio complex and retreat, a twenty-minute drive away in the suburb of Chanhassen. In the Hollywood Hills, the residences of even the most forgettable members of the Brat Pack will have gaggles of nosy parkers pointing a camera at the gates of their homes on a daily, if not hourly, basis. At the childhood residence of Oscar winners and critical darlings the Coen brothers, there's no one.

So unremarkable is this house, so invisible is its history, that any disciple of the Coens who has made the pilgrimage here will linger on the kerbside, checking their notes to make sure they've stopped outside the right place and that their odyssey doesn't end with them taking a picture of the wrong house. If they're lucky, a kindly neighbour might holler confirmation from across the street. 'The Coens? Yah, you got it.' A sense of anticlimax is almost inevitable.

Other than the connection with the pair, this is just another leafy street in another leafy neighbourhood on the outskirts of a city that has a decent amount of leafy streets and leafy neighbourhoods. Safe, homely, unremarkable.

It's exactly the kind of street that Jerry Lundegaard lives on.

And here he comes now, through the front door, a bag of groceries under his arm as he dances out the customary snow-off-the-boots shuffle on the doormat. He's back in the Minneapolis suburbs, back from his out-of-state assignation with Showalter and Grimsrud, back to conceal the peril in which he's just placed his family.

The interior of the Lundegaard homestead mirrors the suburb in which it's set: safe, homely, unremarkable. If they wanted to gently chide anonymous suburban life, to mildly lampoon middle-American taste, the Coens might have overplayed the set design, slightly amplifying the interior decor in the same way that they slightly amplify the Minnesotan accent (more on which later). Instead, the set designer hasn't been asked to plaster the wall with crude cross-stitch designs, nor to assemble armies of tasteless knick-knacks on every available surface. Rather, things have been kept neutral. No comment needs to be made about these people by mocking their living quarters. Let the dialogue do the talking instead.

Jean Lundegaard is furiously chopping celery in the

kitchen. So far, we know her to be a millionaire's daughter – 'She's real wealthy,' Jerry disclosed back in that booth in the King of Clubs – but there's little hint of it here. Her hair looks pretty untended, her clothes decidedly mumsy. And we get no sense of the calm reassurance that long-term financial security can endow. Quite the opposite. Jean seems to be a bag of nerves. Highly strung. A highly strung bag of nerves with a prescription for Valium attached to it.

It's almost as if Jean is a knowing, if not willing, participant of the scheme that's been hatched, that her nervousness is connected to her imminent departure in the trunk of that burnt umber Ciera. (Were she to actually know the fate that her dearly beloved has in store for her, that vegetable slicing would undoubtedly have become even more frenzied.) In time, though, we will discover this manic behaviour, this overload of anxiety, is Jean's default position. The next morning we'll see her frantically stirring a cake mixture while admonishing her son Scotty for his disappointing school grades; later the same day, she'll be knitting at speed when the kidnappers come calling.

After the briefest of pleasantries between husband and wife, the possible source for Jean's nervous unease that evening (and perhaps in life in general) is then revealed in two words. Once these two words leave her mouth, there's silence between the couple for a beat or two – time enough for Jerry's face to look even more put-upon than usual. Any notion of suburban contentment, of a husband returning to his family after a business meeting in another state (albeit a business meeting with a distinctly nefarious agenda), has evaporated. A relaxed evening shall not ensue.

'Dad's here.'

FIVE

THE GUSTAFSON GROWL

Among the three conspirators, Gaear Grimsrud is undoubtedly the alpha male. He's the most physically imposing, the one to be feared, the one whose half-closed eyes you don't want your wide-open-in-fear ones to meet. Thanks to his peroxide hair and ghostly pallor, he resembles a polar bear here in this frozen landscape. Just don't provoke him. Play dead instead.

As he goes about sorting out (or, alternatively, ballsing up) the logistics of the sting, Carl Showalter might think he's calling the shots, but he talks too much. His mouth runs away with him. He's a weasel too – or a 'little fucking weasel', as Shep Proudfoot the mechanic will later call him. And the weasel is an animal that's never at the top of the food chain.

Of course, when it comes to machismo, Showalter still ranks way higher than the emasculated Jerry Lundegaard.

After all, no alpha male walks around with a pair of mittens attached to his coat, coordinating the look with an Elmer Fudd hat. Jerry does.

The target of the conspiracy though – the overbearing business tycoon Wade Gustafson – growls loudest. Literally. It's one of the best sounds of the whole film. Nothing gets to the heart of the frustration with which Wade greets life than the guttural noise produced deep down in the old guy's diaphragm.

In that first scene of his – when, having dropped by his daughter's house, he invites himself for supper – we hear two instances of The Growl. He emits the first as he sits in front of the TV in a tight frenzy, watching his beloved Gophers ice hockey team concede a goal to their big rivals, the University of Wisconsin Badgers, while his left hand pumps away at a stress ball. Later, at the dinner table, The Growl makes another airing, this time articulating Wade's dissatisfaction that grandson Scotty is allowed to leave the table, his dinner half-finished, in order to go and meet his friends at McDonald's. 'What do you think they do there?' grumbles Grandpa. 'They don't drink milkshakes, I assure you!'

Whether to express annoyance at sports teams or at parenting techniques – or, later, at the rules of the ransom handover – The Growl is a sound that encapsulates Wade. He is a man increasingly frustrated with, and confused by, a world that is slipping beyond his control as he slides into pensionable age. This is someone who will have called the plays all of his working life. He's been the quarterback of his business ventures for decades. And The Growl would have been a regular tactic in boardrooms, a device to intimidate and disarm the dealmakers on the other side of the table. Now it's the call of the ageing silverback losing his power.

*

Wade Gustafson has got a well-developed diaphragm. At least Harve Presnell has (or did; he died in 2009). When the Coen brothers cast him as the disagreeable entrepreneur, Presnell's most high-profile film role had been nearly thirty years earlier, alongside Lee Marvin and Clint Eastwood in *Paint Your Wagon*. As Rotten Luck Willie, and with a rich head of hair and sculpted dark beard, he delivered the song 'They Call The Wind Mariah' in the richest of baritones. As a young man, he studied vocal performance and earned a living as an opera singer, often appearing at the Hollywood Bowl, before moving into musical theatre. He played Daddy Warbucks in *Annie* on Broadway for many years, a role for which he was still reporting for duty every night when the Coens came calling.

'I didn't know who they were,' Presnell recalled a couple of years after *Fargo*'s release. 'I don't get out much. Anyway, I met them, which really put me off because they look like derelicts from the late '60s. And they laugh funny. They suck the air in when they laugh, instead of blowing it out. And on top of everything else,' the Californian observed, 'they're from Minneapolis, which is really strange.'

You can imagine the growl of dissatisfaction that Presnell may have let out when he discovered the place of origin of these unsightly longhairs. Perhaps it was that sound that sealed the deal in the brothers' eyes. The Gustafson growl was born.

SIX

'I'M PAYIN' NINETEEN-FIVE FOR THIS VEHICLE HERE!'

The TruCoat scene in the car showroom is one of the neatest of the entire film. Brilliant in its interplay and dialogue, it's also wonderfully self-contained. It's not an open-ended staging post, a junction from which the narrative takes an altered direction. In fact, it doesn't progress the plot a single inch, leaving the kidnapping conspiracy well alone. But there is a very real reason for the scene's existence and inclusion: it's an intense, two-minute character study, a focused light beam aimed at the dark heart of Jerry Lundegaard.

It's still early in the film. Perhaps the morally dubious Jerry will be redeemed by the time the closing credits roll and will have become the hero. Plus, the way that his father-in-law bullies and belittles him – only hinted at so far – could elicit further pity for his plight.

But to see the man at large in his apparently natural

environment of a car showroom is to see the man wearing his true colours. Behind the empty smiles lurks a brain ready to take advantage. Jerry proves himself to be an operator as oily as the mechanics' overalls out back in the bodyshop.

Soundtracked by the hush of the most benign muzak ever conceived (imagine what beige would sound like and you'll be close), we're offered a few establishing shots: a line of box-fresh new vehicles crowned by Gustafson Motors signs on their roofs; a coffee machine that dispenses complimentary beverages; a wall of 8x10 photos of the company's legion of sales executives. Then we're dumped right into the middle of a heated exchange. Or, at least, one side of it.

The customer's voice, an octave higher than sounds natural and in danger of cracking, sets out the parameters of the disagreement. 'I sat right here and said I didn't want any TruCoat.'

Across the desk, Jerry, wearing a pin on his lapel denoting his years of service to the car dealership trade, is as cool as the icy I-394 highway outside his window. He's as in control as we'll see him throughout the entire film.

There's a reason for this. He's been here before. He knows what he's doing. Reneging on an agreed deal in order to squeeze a few dollars more out of a customer – in this case, adding the application of an unwanted sealant and upping the price to the tune of an extra $500 – is what he does all day long. Bending the truth, but stopping short of losing the deal. As the lapel pin confirms, he's well-versed in the dark arts of car sales.

Jerry's defence is rehearsed and easy. It's clearly worked before.

'Yah, but I'm sayin', that TruCoat, you don't get it, you get oxidisation problems. It'll cost you a heck of a lot more'n five hunnert dollars –'

The wronged customer – his wife's under-her-breath attempts to calm him reveal his name to be Bucky – leans forward in his chair. His eyes squint in bemusement. His voice continues to climb.

'We had a deal here for nineteen-five . . .' he protests. 'You called me twenty minutes ago and said you had it! Ready to make delivery, ya says! Come on down and get it! And here you are and you're wasting *my* time and my *wife's* time and I'm payin' nineteen-five for this vehicle here!'

Bucky is gone. Any cool is lost. His arms are gesticulating, his nostrils flaring. Those eyes are now popped open in anger.

But the seasoned salesman – a diffident, submissive character in any other scenario – stands firm. The long-term reputation of both himself and the company goes unconsidered. He doesn't care about keeping Bucky's repeat custom a few years down the line. All he cares about is securing that extra amount, or a significant part of it, right now. He has sales targets, after all.

Jerry disappears into a side-office on the pretext of talking to his boss; instead he has the briefest of conversations with a burger-chomping colleague about the Gophers, before re-emerging with a smile painted on his face. It's the same fake smile that adorns his 8x10 on the wall. He explains how he now has permission to knock a whole hundred dollars off the TruCoat price. 'Well, he never done this before . . .'

It's at this precise point that, were any residue of compassion towards him still held by a single member of the popcorn-munching audience out in the stalls, Jerry wipes it clean away. His gall adds a few drops of kerosene to the fire in that office too.

You get the sense, so strait-laced are this couple, that Bucky hasn't sworn in maybe twenty years. 'You lied to me, Mr Lundegaard. You're a bald-faced liar!'

He pauses, hoping to swallow the profanity that's rising in his throat. It's no good. Out it comes.

'A fucking liar –'

As Bucky roots around in his wife's handbag for his chequebook, Jerry can't hold eye contact any longer; instead he gazes down at the doodles on his notepad and the collection of freshly sharpened pencils on his desk. There's embarrassment at deceiving this couple, sure, but there's also internal shame that he's reduced to such tactics to put a comparatively trifling amount onto his sales sheet. He wants to be a player, but he's still a small-time grifter. Every time he tries this trick, he's left with a bitter aftertaste that reminds him he's no more than a common swindler.

And this is an episode that will rankle with Bucky every time he runs a chamois over the sealant-enhanced bodywork of his new car. It certainly did for Ethan Coen. For, as deliciously scripted and beautifully acted as this two-way is, the choreography of this scene arrived pretty much fully formed, thanks to a past encounter when the younger Coen was looking for a new vehicle. He was that irate customer to whom the salesman was talking in circles, telling bald-faced lies. The scene, he admitted, was 'an almost verbatim transcript of my experience'.

So perfectly nuanced is Gary Houston's turn as Bucky it's a shame he's only on screen for those two minutes. But while William H. Macy, Frances McDormand and Steve Buscemi take the screen time and, later, the plaudits, it's these small, satisfyingly authentic performances around the edges that truly enhance the entire endeavour. Bucky is one such incidental character whose time is brief but whose impact is memorable; Mr Mohra, the police-calling bartender who appears towards the film's climax, is another.

(Macy clearly remembered the quality of Houston's turn. Nearly two decades later, he was a little kinder than Jerry was towards his character, casting and directing him in an episode of the TV comedy-drama *Shameless*.)

As well as confirming Jerry's slipperiness beyond reasonable doubt, the TruCoat scene also shows the disdain that his colleagues have for him, despite – or, perhaps, because of – his position as executive sales manager. That awkward exchange with the colleague with the burger will later be replicated in the bodyshop with another lunch-eating Gustafson Motors employee. There's no rapport there, no interaction that's anything more than surface-deep.

He has no allies, no comrades. Even in his most natural habitat – his father-in-law's car dealership – Jerry Lundegaard is a man alone.

SEVEN

THE ODD COUPLE

Let's spare a thought for Gaear Grimsrud. No, really. We must. For a couple of minutes, at least.

Imagine you're the one trapped in the passenger seat of an Oldsmobile Cutlass Ciera for several hours at a stretch, with only hundreds of miles of featureless prairie to look at and the inane witterings of a chatterbox filling your ears. Losing yourself in a fug of cigarette smoke as you ceaselessly make your way through an entire pack of Marlboro is understandable. Anything to keep the nerves level. Anything to neutralise the desire to bludgeon the driver to a bloody, indistinguishable pulp, one that's only identifiable by dental records. (In toothy Showalter's case, what a set of records those must be.)

Perhaps he deserves our praise for holding out as long as he does.

Showalter and Grimsrud are one of cinema's oddest couples: the gobby, fidgety one who thinks he's in charge, and the silent hulk who feels no need to take the lead but who, through his barbarity, shows he has the upper hand. Neither of them give two shits about other people – it's just that Showalter lets everyone know about it, while Grimsrud doesn't. He lets those fearsome eyes do his talking. For him, the main function of a mouth is smoking, not speaking.

(A quick aside: the actors themselves are both the opposites of their characters, as Peter Stormare – aka Grimsrud – explained to the *Examiner*. 'Steve Buscemi, in between takes, becomes like a clam. It's hard to get a word out of him. It's very funny. He's not actually a big talker in between takes, but I am. I like to talk to the crew and blah, blah, blah. He's very quiet – a quiet little guy.')

Fargo, a film with dysfunction coursing through its arteries – deceit, shallowness, dumb decisions, unjustified violence – is personified by Showalter and Grimsrud. It's their ill-advised, illogical actions that tilt events off course, that dictate the calamitous direction of the plot. So erratic is their behaviour that they're even capable of making Jerry Lundegaard seem a paragon of reason and rationality.

Despite their differences, the mismatched pair do occupy some common ground. Not only do they believe that the accumulation of money trumps the sanctity and preservation of life, they will also show that they are united in their lack of professionalism, in reacting in a hot-headed manner when things don't go quite to plan. As such, they represent what Ethan Coen identified as 'our desire to go against the Hollywood cliché of the bad guy as a super-professional who controls everything he does. In fact, in most cases, criminals belong to the strata of society least equipped to face life, and that's the reason they're caught so often.'

Showalter and Grimsrud should be able to marshal their respective experience to carry out the job with the minimum fuss and disruption. But they seem to have jettisoned any expertise they might have amassed over their respective criminal careers. Perhaps they see the assignment as sufficiently straightforward that they don't need to have a grand plan, that they'll busk it, rolling with any punches that come their way. Their myopia, and their lack of communication, means they've even failed to address how to split the Ciera once the job's done. This will, of course, have grave consequences for one of them.

There is no joint plan of action, no dovetailing of roles. Throughout, we see that Grimsrud in particular operates independently. He's a lone wolf. A loose cannon. Even if there were a script, he would disregard it, or burn holes in it with the tip of his Marlboro.

In *Pulp Fiction*, the equivalent double act – Samuel L. Jackson's Jules Winnfield and John Travolta's Vincent Vega – have a genuine connection: they're a partnership who shoot from the same hymn sheet. Or, at least, adhere to the same Bible passage: namely Ezekiel 25:17. 'And I will strike down upon thee with great vengeance and furious anger . . .'

And there's a personal rapport. Winnfield and Vega converse. They connect. They're continually riffing, their conversations sharp and alive with subjects that range far and wide, from the names of internationally available hamburgers to the hidden meaning of foot massages or the cleanliness (or otherwise) of pigs. By comparison, Showalter and Grimsrud have nothing. They feel like strangers who were introduced just an hour or so before Jerry's snowy boots shuffled into the King of Clubs.

Just what is their connection? Had they done time behind bars together? Were they cellmates? Had they carried out past jobs in the same dysfunctional, lop-sided manner? Or could Grimsrud – the one first approached to take on the kidnapping, despite Showalter's outward appearance as the duo's leader – find no better person among the criminal underworld in the city of Fargo to front up the operation, to do the talking? It's never revealed.

In the opening scene in the Fargo bar, Showalter had the air of someone professional, someone efficient. His demeanour was controlled. Focused on the job, eyes on the prize. Of the three, he was clearly the one in command.

Now, on the open road, at the wheel of that straight-off-the-forecourt Ciera, there are distractions. It's not simply a drive down to Minneapolis and the Lundegaard homestead. First, Showalter needs to find somewhere to get a shot and a beer and a steak. Somewhere to get laid too. Meanwhile Grimsrud, being such a wholesome fellow, is holding out for pancakes. (He's not averse to getting laid, though.)

However, any post-coital satisfaction is short-lived. After their dalliances with a pair of hookers at the Blue Ox motel (another sign of their confusing relationship is being able to share a twin room while they attend to their needs with their respective sexual partners), the tension hangs heavy in the car the following morning as they approach Minneapolis. You could blame it on pre-kidnap nerves, were this not par for the course for how they interact. Or, rather, how they don't.

Showalter is giving Grimsrud a primer lesson about the Minneapolis skyline, pointing out the all-glass IDS Building. The Swede is utterly disinterested, and his disdain for his partner is clear. Clear to everyone but Showalter, that is.

'Shit, I'm sittin' here driving, doin' all the driving, man, whole fucking way from Brainerd, drivin', just tryin' to chat, you know, keep our spirits up, fight the boredom of the road, and you can't say one fuckin' thing just in the way of conversation?'

Silence. Grimsrud, memorably labelled by the doyen of American film critics Roger Ebert as 'a sullen slug of few words', continues to stare out of the window. He's presumably contemplating – like us – how and why he ever teamed up with this loudmouth.

'Well, fuck it, I don't have to talk either, man. See how you like it.'

The silence continues. No reaction.

'Just total fuckin' silence. Two can play at that game, smart guy. We'll just see how you like it . . .'

A beat.

Another beat.

'Total silence . . .'

EIGHT

'HE SAYS IT'S PRETTY SWEET . . .'

There's not a lot of sunshine around in midwinter Minnesota. And there's not a lot of sunshine in Jerry Lundegaard's life, whatever the season.

If, with graph paper and a pen, you plotted his fortunes during these most significant days in his underwhelming life, you would be tracing an almost exclusively downward slope. Towards the end of the graph, the angle of decline would get steeper as the unravelling of the conspiracy gained pace.

Earlier on, though, close to the left-hand margin, you would be able to plot a slight upturn in the way things are going for him, the mildest of parabolas. It doesn't last long, just a few hours, but it does beam a little warmth and light into his soulless life.

It's breakfast-time at the Lundegaards' house and Wade is on the phone. He's his usual gruff self, ignoring the small talk and getting straight to business. But there's the very slight hint of softness at the edges. It seems that Jerry's parking-lot venture carries some weight. 'Stan Grossman looked at your proposal. He says it's pretty sweet . . .'

If Wade's uber-cautious right-hand man has taken his foot off the brake, it could just be that Jerry has played his cards right. A smile – one of the very few genuine smiles to grace Jerry's face – breaks out.

A meeting is arranged.

'Come by two-thirty.'

Jerry now has a date with the rest of his life. It's not just that his money woes might be over. He now also appears to have finally impressed his father-in-law after being a perpetual disappointment ever since Jean introduced them to each other. This is the most relaxed that we will ever see him. It's no coincidence that, right now, he's yet to button up his work shirt or put on his tie. He'll soon be properly dressed, though. Buttoned right up. Unable to breathe so easily.

Jerry looks out of the kitchen window, perhaps towards a brave new tomorrow. We're suspicious, though. The film's only twelve minutes in and we've yet to see a drop of that bloodshed that the poster in the lobby promised. There aren't going to be any happy endings just yet. Chances are there won't be one at all. Come on, Jerry. Drop the smile. Have you never *seen* a film before?

Once he arrives at work, Jerry struts across the garage floor to talk to Shep Proudfoot, the mechanic who put him in touch with Grimsrud. Jerry's aim is to call off the kidnapping, now that Plan A appears to be heading towards fruition, but he can't get hold of the pair. As we know, by this juncture they're already on their way towards snatching Jean. And this is 1987. Cell phones have yet to reach upstate Minnesota.

One-way awkward bonhomie ensues as the monosyllabic Proudfoot can't help Jerry (and he wouldn't anyway). Retreating back to the sales floor, Jerry perhaps entertains the thought that he could get hold of two separate piles of Wade's cash – effectively going through with both Plan A and Plan B. Or perhaps he simply parks the idea of intervening in the kidnapping for now. Either way, nothing is going to put an obstacle in the way of that afternoon's potentially life-changing meeting with Wade.

The smile, though, will soon disappear. The line on the graph will head downwards again. And it will never stop.

NINE

WHY DOES JERRY NEED ALL THIS MONEY?

'Mr Lundegaard? This is Reilly Diefenbach from GMAC. How are you this morning?'

The next couple of minutes aren't going to go well for Jerry. Here, back in his tiny office at Gustafson Motors, scene of innumerable mistreatments of his customers, it's the oily salesman who's going to feel stitched up.

Straight away we suspect that the ensuing conversation, with this representative from the General Motors Acceptance Corporation, won't deliver good news for Jerry. Nor will he go up in our estimation by the end of the call. Instead, the exchange will provide further evidence that he is one slippery critter. It reveals someone forever evading the consequences of the decisions he's made, sidestepping the trouble he's got himself into.

Jerry tries to charm the GMAC man, switching on the easy, superficial tone that he greets his customers with, but

Diefenbach isn't playing ball. He won't be diverted from his task at hand. He needs clarification on a number of cars against which Jerry appears to have secured a hefty loan, but he can't read the serial numbers on the fax application. There's a reason for the GMAC man cutting to the quick and not indulging in pleasantries. This is a properly large loan. Three hundred and twenty thousand dollars, in fact. That large.

And, if Jerry's taking out a loan of that scale in addition to cheating Wade out of what we will learn to be the best part of a million dollars, it's some serious financial shit he's in.

He appears to be not so much up to his neck in debt, but to have actually slipped below the surface and submerged at speed. Not only is Jerry trying to forge a big-bucks deal with his father-in-law to help clear his debts, and not only is he trying to extort the same family member, but it appears, from his current evasiveness, that he's also defrauding the finance arm of General Motors. This is a man who's certainly not timid nor unambitious when it comes to picking his targets.

This was one plan that Jerry thought had already come off. He reassures Diefenbach that the loans are in place. The money may have reached his account last month, but he hadn't factored in a subsequent GMAC audit. His face drops with the realisation that he's no longer in the clear. It drops even further when he's informed that, if the numbers can't be correlated with specific vehicles, the money will be recalled. Jerry puts the phone down. He's deeper into the mire.

The framing of this single-camera scene adds plenty to the feeling that Jerry is imprisoned by his financial affairs. The camera watches him from outside his office, from the sales floor. The window is partially obscured by half-closed vertical blinds, and we can see that the other window, separating his office from the outside world, has its blinds in a similar half-closed position. These are effectively prison bars, isolating Jerry, enclosing him. This is his cell. He's doing solitary. But, of course, it's self-imprisonment. He's the author of what may well be his own downfall.

But why the downfall? He lives in a comfortable house in a comfortable part of town. And, as the executive sales manager of Gustafson Motors, he has a – presumably – decently paid job. When did things start becoming uncomfortable? What events have occurred to put him in this perilous state, to force him to dream up a series of elaborate ruses in an attempt to balance his personal books? In short, how come he owes all this money?

The Coens give us no inkling about the nature of the debt, either its exact size (although we know it's eye-wateringly vast) or, more pointedly, the cause of it. The only reference to the hole in Jerry's finances was in that opening scene in the King of Clubs when he mumbled something about 'personal matters that needn't, uh . . .'

That wasn't just a shifty car salesman telling the kidnappers to butt out of his affairs. This was also the Coens telling the audience that they weren't going to spell out every detail of the story. They're not chapter-and-verse merchants, after all. They'll never spoon-feed. The audience don't need to know the cause. They just need to know that Jerry is in a whole heap of trouble. Nothing more.

Still, it's fun to speculate.

Perhaps he hadn't been hitting his sales targets for a good long time and had only been bringing home a meagre, bonus-free basic wage that didn't cover the essential outgoings of domestic life. It's certainly plausible that, thanks to his position as executive sales manager, he could cover up his failings, but this must have been going on for years and years to get anywhere close to the depth of debt he appears to have amassed, a black hole in his finances that needs many hundreds of thousands of dollars to fill it.

Perhaps someone is trying to extort Jerry (which may in turn have been the inspiration for his own plan to extort Wade). One reason for this might be a sexual indiscretion that he doesn't want to stain his home life. But it's difficult to see Jerry as a sexual animal. We appreciate he's capable of deceiving a loved one, but his desirability to anyone beyond mousey Jean is questionable. Similarly, it's unlikely that this schmuck has developed a drug habit that's hoovering up cash.

We know Jerry doesn't have expensive tastes. He has no eye for expensive suits or shoes, outfits that wouldn't, of course, be up to what a Minnesotan winter would throw at them. He's happy enough in his parka and snow boots. And we've seen the decor of his home; no silly money is being squandered there on a bank-breaking collection of high art.

The best bet is that Jerry is up to his neck in gambling debts, that an endless series of credit cards have been maxed out in pursuit of that one big payday. This is the most plausible reason: an attempt to add some colour to his drab, beige life and to step out of his father-in-law's shadow to be the man to provide for his wife and child. Wade has already made it clear that Jean and Scotty will never have to worry about their long-term financial future. But Jerry wants to be the one to say that.

Whatever the cause, whatever the decision or series of decisions that he's made and that have put him in the desperate place he now occupies, you can bet that – with the dogged Diefenbach on his tail – Jerry now regrets every bad move he ever made.

Sinking fast and with his options reducing, he will soon realise those waters get even deeper once a certain pair of kidnappers develop itchy trigger fingers.

TEN

THE KIDNAP

Abduction has always been – and, as long as cameras are aimed at actors, probably always will be – a staple of the movies. From the first-ever Western (1899's *Kidnapping by Indians*) to Liam Neeson's seemingly endless, and endlessly violent, pursuit of the abductors of his various family members in the *Taken* series, it's a plot set-up that hasn't weakened over time.

As long as a film-maker presents their abduction in an innovative, unhackneyed way, they're on to a winner. The conflict is in-built. It's there right from the act itself: that three-way tension between the kidnapper, the kidnapped and the payer of the ransom. An abduction also provides the means via which a director can put as much, or as little, action and violence into their film as they like, whether during the kidnapping, during the period of a hostage's captivity, or to resolve the entire endeavour. As

Joel Coen says, 'a kidnapping is pregnant with dramatic possibilities'.

Certainly, the Coens keep returning to abductions as the pivot of their plots. 'We seem to like kidnapping stories,' says Joel with a shrug. Whether successful, failed or faked, abductions have featured in five of their films. But, thanks to the way that the brothers shift their shape to work in different genres – be they noir or thriller or screwball comedy – any similarity between the premise is obscured by the tone in which it unfolds. They make it as heavy or as light as they wish.

And, of course, no Coen kidnapping goes to plan. The linear narrative of victim kidnapped/ransom demanded/ ransom paid/victim released satisfies neither the mind of the film-maker nor the mind of the viewer. It's just a case of whether the plan falls to bits in comical fashion or in a pool of blood.

The plot of their first feature film, *Blood Simple*, included the attempted kidnap of an estranged wife by her husband. Although a catalyst for the plot twists that were to follow (the failed abduction led to the husband commissioning a hitman), the thwarted abduction is not the pivot around which the rest of the movie rotates.

The Coens' follow-up, 1987's *Raising Arizona*, is all about the kidnap, though. And a literal kidnap it is too – the snatching of a baby, from a prominent family who've just had quintuplets, by a childless couple. 'They had more'n they could handle' is their justification. The first kidnap attempt, by Nicolas Cage's ex-con character Hi McDunnough, is aborted. 'They started cryin', then they were all over me,' he whines to his prison officer wife Ed, played by Holly Hunter. 'It was kinda horrifying.' His second attempt is more successful, but the couple are soon the victims of a kidnapping themselves. Former cellmates of Hi snatch the baby, albeit only after a high-comedy fight in Hi's trailer between him and John Goodman's character Gale Snoats.

The abduction of a minor would be a harrowing subject were this a seat-edge thriller or a taut noir. But as we're in the realms of knockabout comedy, our alarm is diverted by the ineptness of the scrap between Hi and Gale. Heads bang on low-hanging lightshades, punches fly through chipboard walls, hands are burned on lightbulbs.

The abduction of a millionaire's trophy wife, and the subsequent ransom demands, were a central plank of 1998's

The Big Lebowski. Or, at least, the *suspected* abduction. Either way, it ensured that – via a case of mistaken identity – The Dude, Jeff Bridges' White Russian-sipping stoner, was mixed up in all the subsequent intricacies and double-crossings, usually to his blank bemusement. There was clear shared territory with *Fargo*, the Coen film which immediately preceded it. Not only was the ransom a million dollars, but the demand also called for 'no funny stuff', echoing Jerry Lundegaard's insistence that Jean's abduction was to be 'a no-rough-stuff-type deal'. But because the darkness of *Fargo* was at the opposite end of the spectrum from *The Big Lebowski*'s Californian sunshine, the similarities managed to keep their distance. No accusations of repetition were heard.

Perhaps, at this point, the Coens realised they were sailing too close to the wind. They went a full eighteen years before resurrecting the kidnap theme in 2016's *Hail, Caesar!* Again, this was a light-hearted take on the subject. Covering a day in the life of a 1950s Hollywood fixer, one of its plotlines involved the drugging and abduction of a dim-witted leading man by a cabal of Communist screenwriters. They demanded a ransom from the studio, not suspecting that the actor would be promptly converted to their cause. A Hollywood kidnapping did, though, prompt a great tagline: 'Lights. Camera. Abduction.'

The taking of Jean Lundegaard is, by the longest Minnesotan country mile, the most brutal of all the Coens' kidnaps. While it is a scene with the odd lighter moment that might raise the slightest of chuckles – for instance, when Grimsrud elects to attend to his injured hand rather than get on with the job from which he's going to pocket twenty grand – its brutality is undeniable.

The domestic peace of the scene's opening only amplifies the chaos about to ensue. Jean is on the sofa, knitting while watching her favourite mid-morning TV show. Muffled footsteps can be heard on the snowy stairs outside, leading up from the backyard. A figure, hooded and carrying a crowbar, appears at the top of them. At this point, Jean is still watching him with curiosity. Only when the window is violently pierced by the crowbar does she leap from the sofa in terror – a terror that's doubled when a second man, also hooded, bursts through the front door to apprehend her.

We see a different Jean in this scene: a tenacious, resolute Jean. Until now, she's been the compliant housewife, the eager-to-please daughter. Now she's a fighter, sinking her teeth deeply into Grimsrud's hand as he tries to muzzle her. This is an echo of the failed abduction in *Blood Simple*, where that estranged wife, Abby (played by Frances McDormand), twists back her abductee's finger while his hand also muzzles her. Jean, though, unlike Abby, doesn't have the foresight to deliver a smart kick to her assailant's nether regions. She's too busy fleeing up the stairs.

However, Jean does have the presence of mind to grab her bedside phone before disappearing into the en-suite bathroom – although this is violently wrenched from her hands when the cable is yanked from the other side of the door. She then leaves the window open, as if that was her point of exit. Showalter takes the bait and heads back outside. It's only Grimsrud's determination to find medication ('I need unguent') that alerts him, via the medicine cabinet's mirror, to Jean hiding behind the shower curtain.

For those able to sidestep the scene's brutality, there may be more chuckles to be had as Jean, blinded by the curtain that's been ripped from its rings, bounces off wardrobes, lamps and door frames as she tries to make her getaway.

She falls spectacularly down the stairs, backwards, rolling and tumbling like an old tyre on a bumpy slope. She could have sustained injuries far more serious than any bumps and bruises she might have received from Showalter and Grimsrud bundling her into the Ciera. Grimsrud knows this, prodding her prone body at the bottom of the stairs, looking for signs of life.

Any laughter has stopped.

ELEVEN

THE FACE OF MACY

Summoned to that post-lunch meeting with Wade and unable to get in touch with Grimsrud and Showalter, Jerry still has a chance to stop the kidnapping taking place. He could put off his father-in-law until tomorrow, park his car down the block from his house and intervene when the Ciera turned the corner into the street. Simply cancel the booking and let the pair ride off into the tundra with a new car in their possession. No harm done, no violent crime committed. Jean need never know.

But he doesn't. We can only guess that the greedy so-and-so has decided to squeeze both chunks of money from Wade: the loan and the ransom.

Despite knowing that he'll be coming back to an empty house that evening – but not knowing what Jean's snatching actually entails – Jerry fixes his gaze on the money instead, positively skipping into his father-in-law's office. He's ready to receive some good news – news of a sufficiently good nature that he may be able to finally climb out of that undiagnosed financial hole.

Jerry rarely, if ever, smiles in Wade's company, but here he's wearing the broadest of ear-to-ear beams that William H. Macy can muster. The schmuck's troubles just might be over. More than that, he's starting to fulfil the billing he wants for himself. With the signing of this deal to put a parking lot in a prime location out in Wayzata, he'll now be a business partner of his all-powerful father-in-law. A player.

Or so he thinks. The fact that there's no chair for him to sit on in the office – instead he's forced to perch on the back of an armchair – hints that this isn't quite going to be how things pan out, that he's not among equals. He just might not be a winner after all.

Macy is at his best playing losers, walking with a world-weary shuffle, shifting his face into the most downbeat frown imaginable. As Little Bill in *Boogie Nights*, released the year after *Fargo*, he was the assistant director whose porn-star wife bedded another man, quite possibly because of the inadequacies her husband's nickname hinted at. All three fell victim to Bill's handgun, the lovers executed in a dispassionate *Fargo*-esque manner before he took care of himself.

Six years later, Macy took lead billing in *The Cooler*, playing another schmuck, Bernie Lootz, a man who has made a career of his inherent loserness. He works for a casino, bringing his innate bad luck to bear by visiting tables where punters are on a winning streak. He shambles in, hangs around to see their fortunes change, and shambles away again – a sad sack in a suit several sizes too big.

Not graced with matinee-idol looks, Macy is one of Hollywood's great character actors. He has an extraordinary face, wide in the mouth and with those flinty blue eyes that can switch from innocent to shifty in a blink. And there's no scene in the whole of *Fargo* where Macy uses that face to arguably the greatest effect than the one in Wade's office.

Nine words kill his buoyant mood.

'What kind of finder's fee were you looking for?' barks Wade.

Jerry's smile freezes. Those eyes widen with uncertainty. Confusion reigns. 'Huh?'

Stan Grossman, Wade's right-hand man, the counterweight to his boss's belligerence, helps out. 'The financials are pretty thorough, so the only thing we don't know is your fee.'

Jerry's face heads south, the euphoria draining from it. 'I was bringin' you this deal for you to loan *me* the money to put in. It's my deal here, see?'

In attempting to occupy the same business strata as Wade and Stan, Jerry has misunderstood the rules of engagement. In a matter of seconds, his new business partners are no longer his new business partners. In fact, they're laughing at his wet-behind-the-ears proposal. 'We're not a bank, Jerry,' Stan informs him more than once.

From being frozen by confusion, Jerry's face dissolves into a series of tics as he desperately tries to gain some traction for his proposal. One of his two big plans (is it Plan A or Plan B?) is unravelling. His head shakes, nervous smiles make fleeting appearances, his blinking becomes more rapid. Disjointed words tumble out of his mouth.

The other two are having none of it. Jerry momentarily bows his head, resetting his face. He looks his father-in-law in the eye, now deathly serious, and guarantees that they'll get their money back.

No dice. The pair then announce their plans to make a move on the deal, 'innapendently'.

Jerry is crestfallen. And few actors can do crestfallen like William H. Macy.

He wasn't the obvious person to cast as Jerry. Unlike Marge and Showalter, characters created with the specific actors in mind, the Coens hadn't yet envisaged a particular person to fill Jerry's snow boots. In fact, when they cast Macy, they almost surprised themselves; Jerry turned out to be quite different from their original idea of him. 'He is neat and tidy,' explained Joel, 'not how we envisioned him. We imagined him as sloven, uncomfortable in his body, a little overweight. Casting Bill, we went in the other direction. He is very put together, but tight and repressed.'

The critic Roger Ebert agreed that Macy was perfectly cast, an actor with the chops to create 'the unbearable agony of a man who needs to think fast, and whose brain is scrambled with fear, guilt and the crazy illusion that he can somehow still pull this thing off'.

The consensus is that it proved to be an inspired casting, but the Coens initially needed some persuasion about Macy's suitability. He'd already read the part for them (to strong effect, he thought), but then discovered other actors were being road-tested, as he recalled to *Entertainment Weekly*. 'I found out that they were auditioning in New York still, so I got my jolly, jolly Lutheran ass on an airplane and walked in and said, "I want to read again because I'm scared you're going to screw this up and hire someone else." I actually said that. You know, you can't play that card too often as an actor. Sometimes it just blows up in your face. But I said, "Guys, this is my role. I want this."' Macy also jokingly threatened to kill Ethan Coen's recently acquired dog.

It's difficult to consider anyone else conveying Jerry's frustration in quite the same brilliant way that Macy does. Suitably chastised after the meeting in Wade's office, he trudges back to his car – an astounding aerial shot from cinematographer Roger Deakins that emphasises this failing man's utter isolation. His is the only car in the large parking lot, now covered in a fresh coating of snow.

'We had fifty cars that we were going to put into the parking lot,' Deakins later explained. 'But we got in in the morning and set up the camera and just one truck had gone through to leave that one tyre track. I said to Joel,

"Let's not have any more cars. It's just a great graphic – this little figure and this one car in this empty lot.'"

Everything is conspiring against Jerry. A thick layer of ice needs scraping off the windshield, the seesawing action of which causes him to have a meltdown. He throws down the ice scraper, his arms waving wildly in uncontrollable frustration. His escape route has been blocked. Then, the quickest of glances upwards to Wade's office several storeys up, hoping that no one has witnessed his tantrum.

Deakins loved it. 'That was just one take. He just had it.'

'That's the way I lose it,' Macy confirmed, again referring to his religious upbringing. 'I'm Lutheran. I rarely blow, but when I do, it has nothing to do with reality. It looks like that – ineffectual and kind of silly.'

In that parking lot, that's just how the last fifteen minutes have made Jerry Lundegaard feel. Ineffectual and kind of silly. Never a player.

Only a single roll of the dice is left. It's now up to the kidnappers to carry out the plan as commissioned, to save this sad sap from the pit of financial ruin.

TWELVE

THE GREAT PRETENDER

Jerry's frustration at Wade rejecting his business proposal seems to have thawed a little. We're probably an hour or so on from his hissy fit in the parking lot, as he steps across the threshold of the Lundegaard house. Scotty's not home from school yet, and Jerry's had time to stop off at the supermarket on the way back from his humiliation up in Wade's office. With two bags of food shopping under his arms, he performs that same snow-boot shuffle on the doormat. And there's that same call-out to his wife so she's not alarmed at his sudden entrance. 'Hon? Got the growshries . . .'

Of course, Jean's already been extremely alarmed at a sudden entrance today. Whether Jerry knows at this point that the abduction has happened is unclear. He might genuinely be calling out to Jean, believing her to be in her usual spot in the kitchen, pursuing one of her favourite hobbies, either frantically chopping vegetables or whipping up some cake mixture, arms blurred like the wings of a hummingbird.

Or Jerry may well know exactly when Jean was going to be kidnapped and is thus going through the motions of pretending it's just another normal day in the Minneapolis suburbs. If so, he's doing it to an audience of no one but himself. He'll have surely played this scene out in his head several times in the last few days. Or, at least, while walking the aisles of the supermarket ten minutes ago. But then Jerry spies the debris of what was clearly anything but a straightforward abduction. This wasn't in the plan.

With the groceries still in his arms, he walks slowly through the house, surveying the devastation, his numbed brain trying to work out the sequence of events. The en-suite bathroom in particular is a bomb site. The contents of the medicine cabinet – the result of Grimsrud's hunt for unguent – are scattered across a counter top. Plastic shower-curtain rings litter the floor next to the pink handset of the telephone; a couple of small remnants of the shower curtain itself still hang from the rail. The door is splintered around the lock. The window is open, and its fly screen lies on the floor, dented. Next to it, hinting at the violent nature of the incident that caused this mess, is Showalter's crowbar.

It's clear to anyone, even someone with spectacularly low levels of deduction, that something very bad has happened here. There has been an almighty struggle and an attempted escape, almost certainly thwarted. Even semi-detached Jerry, super-superficial Jerry, understands the gravity of the situation. What had he expected, though? That Jean would have put down her knitting and gone quietly, compliantly?

At this point, Carter Burwell's score accompanies Jerry's survey of the crime scene, its gentle tone offering a suggestion that he might now do the right thing, that he'll now step into the light. He wanted to call the whole plan off before. Now's the time he should really do so. This is a moral test.

He fails. Instead of making a U-turn onto the path of (albeit fractional) righteousness, he chooses to continue his passage down the wrong road. At least he's consistent in that: by now, we expect every choice to be a bad choice. Now that the legitimate deal with Wade has faded and the GMAC have his card marked, there's only one option: to go through with the ransom demand.

And, let's face it, had Jerry made the morally correct decision, this would be a substantially shorter film. Instead, we get to take a further measure of his gross inhumanity as he compounds his fate even further. And it's an inhumanity underscored by an innate dimness, as the man who inhabited Jerry's body was at pains to point out. 'The guy's as stupid as a bag of rocks,' Macy observed. 'Everything he touched just went to hell.'

In the next shot, as the camera pans over the shower curtain, still lying in a pool at the bottom of the stairs, to show the smashed window in the living room, the audience can hear this bag-of-rocks-stupid man putting a call in to Wade, his voice apparently quivering in fear and agitation.

'Yah, Wade, I – it's Jerry, I . . .'

Then a variation, more anguished: 'Wade, it's Jerry. I don't know what to do. It's Jean. I don't know what to do. It's my wife. I don't know what to do. It's Jean. . .'

Then the killer reveal, the shot that confirms the jet blackness of Jerry's heart. He's standing in the kitchen, but he's not actually on the phone. He's merely rehearsing the correct tone to take when informing Wade that his daughter has been abducted. The debris strewn throughout the house has, ultimately, had little effect on him. Instead he's having to fake that anguish. He is an actor, an emotionless carcass, an empty shell. Nothing seems to affect him. To borrow from a later Coen brothers work, Jerry Lundegaard is the man who isn't there.

There are a couple more practice runs, in which he varies the words used – 'Oh geez, it's terrible' – before he finally picks up the phone. He reaches the receptionist at Wade's office. His voice snaps back to its normal cadence and tone, as if nothing remotely untoward has happened. Certainly, it's not the voice of someone who's just discovered his wife has been violently kidnapped.

'Er, yeah, Wade Gustafson, please.'

The scumbag.

THIRTEEN

'WHOA DADDY . . .'

Fargo could never be described as an action movie. Despite a medium-sized body count, its pace only occasionally accelerates beyond sedentary. The moviegoers of 1996 would have had to relocate to another movie theatre if they had wanted more wall-to-wall, high-action thrills. Tom Cruise's first *Mission: Impossible* flick perhaps, or the tornado-chasing thriller *Twister*. These are films that would never contemplate including seemingly banal scenes about car sealants or finance agreements. *Fargo* would. And did.

So, when it serves up moments of brutal action, we sit up and take notice. And these moments happen suddenly, such as those first homicides out on that snow-encrusted highway. We barely have time to strap ourselves in before the film's cast is three lives lighter.

The tan Ciera, with Showalter still at the wheel, has reached Brainerd on its way back from Minneapolis – or, at least, it's reached the darkness on the edge of town. With a whimpering abductee on the back seat, Showalter and Grimsrud have wisely chosen to steer clear of the usual and quickest route between Minneapolis and Brainerd. This is – as any devotee of the road maps of Minnesota will tell you – the dual carriageway of Route 10 past Elk River and St Cloud, switching to State Highway 371 in Little Falls for the last thirty miles.

But that could potentially be too conspicuous a route, especially if the Lundegaards' neighbours had witnessed, or at least heard, the crash-bang-wallop of what turned out not to be history's quietest kidnapping. And if those neighbours had seen an unusual car in the neighbourhood, taking that particular route might make it difficult to evade the attention of law-enforcement officers prowling up and down those more populated roads.

Instead, it's slower but anonymous single-lane blacktops all the way as they take their hostage north to their hideout under the cover of night. So, it makes it all the more unfortunate when the revolving red lights of a state trooper's car appear in Showalter's rear-view mirror. Even this lonesome highway, past the midnight hour, gets patrolled.

Showalter pulls over. The state trooper pulls over. The situation, understandably, makes Jean – tied up, gagged and with a sack over her head in the back seat – start whimpering again. (She had already been ordered by Grimsrud, in the longest sentence we'll hear him utter in the entire film, to 'shut the fuck up or I'll throw you back into the trunk, you know'. He's endured hours of Showalter's drivel – equal parts bitching and inanity – but it's the perfectly justified sobs of the true victim of the entire scheme that finally crack Grimsrud.)

As the trooper sits in his car, jotting down the Ciera's licence plate, Showalter again tries to play the leader. He's realised that he hasn't attached tags: the stickers affixed to licence plates to show the car has been registered for that calendar year, not dissimilar to road tax in the UK. He says he'll take care of it.

Grimsrud glares across at Showalter, their faces partly illuminated by the headlights of the state trooper's car behind them. This is the first time we've seen concern on Grimsrud's face – aside, that is, from the visible anxiety he showed when it appeared he might not be able to feed his pancake habit at a moment's notice.

Showalter can see the concern. 'Hey!' he repeats. 'I'll take care of this!'

Showalter understands that nullifying the trooper's interest in the dodgy-looking pair and their curiously box-fresh vehicle requires both calmness and charm. And he's fully aware that these are qualities not possessed by his silent partner. He knows how short his associate's fuse is.

The officer approaches, the beam of his flashlight first falling on Showalter and then picking out Grimsrud in the passenger seat. The Swede doesn't help the cause here. We wouldn't expect him to welcome the trooper with an ear-to-ear grin or to engage him in dazzling repartee, but he couldn't look more like a murderous psychopath if he tried. Those dead eyes refuse to look in the trooper's direction, while that obligatory Marlboro defies gravity as it hangs from his lips.

After the flashlight's beam briefly scans the back seat, the trooper enquires whether this is a new car, inviting Showalter to go on the charm offensive.

'Oh, it certainly is, officer. Still got that smell!'

He allows himself a smirk, but his attempt at humour falls on deaf ears. The monotone of the trooper's voice is the sound of a straight-bat, law-upholding jobsworth. He doesn't do chat. Showalter's bid to bring levity to the situation has failed. He'll try another tactic instead. When prompted, he offers up his licence and registration, carefully allowing a fifty-dollar note to protrude from his wallet.

Bad move. Until then, the trooper had no real reason, save for Grimsrud's surly demeanour, to believe anything was particularly untoward. By offering a bribe where no bribe need be offered, Showalter has now alerted the trooper that the pair are involved in something shady, something that needs covering up. Grimsrud swallows hard. It's at this point that he knows the trooper isn't going to get out of this situation alive.

The wallet returned, with the fifty-dollar bill intact, the trooper – in the last words of his life – commands Showalter to step out of the car. She might be blind to the events, but Jean can hear it's taken a turn for the worse. She's already been threatened with being shot, so she knows there are firearms on board. Her muted squeal can be interpreted as an attempt to warn the trooper that he's in grave danger.

And Jean is absolutely right. As his flashlight seeks the source of the noise, Grimsrud reaches across Showalter to slam the trooper's head into the window frame of the driver's door. Holding him with one hand, the other reaches into the glove compartment, pulls out a pistol and despatches the trooper with a single shot to the head. A fountain of blood spurts into Showalter's lap. Even he's shocked by the suddenness and severity of events. 'Whoa . . . Whoa, Daddy.'

This is the point at which the covers are pulled off the kidnappers' relationship, the point at which the true power is unveiled. Until now, Showalter's fast and loose tongue has led proceedings. Grimsrud, despite having earlier been revealed by Shep Proudfoot as Jerry's initial point of contact, has until now been regarded by the audience as just the muscle, the enforcer. Now he's the one making the decisions; whether these are advisable ones or otherwise is up for debate, but not right now. This was a time for action. Resolution had been needed when it came to the state trooper. To a killer's worldview, there was no other way out – not after Showalter's attempted bribe and Jean's warning.

Confirmation that Grimsrud is now calling the shots comes with his instruction to Showalter to move the trooper's body from the highway. Is this a moment of compassion from the Swede, saving the corpse from being run over by other vehicles? Why not leave the body in situ and get the hell out of there as fast as possible? After all, the longer Showalter takes to drag the body onto the verge, the longer the pair will remain at the crime scene – and the higher the chance of them being implicated in the killing, even if they are several miles past the back of beyond in the soot-black dead of a winter's night.

And so it proves. Headlights appear on the black horizon. A car approaches, slowing as it reaches the scene. Its two occupants gaze across, wide-mouthed, and soak up the sight: a patently dead state trooper being hauled off the highway. The driver hits the gas. Another Grimsrud decision. Another no-other-way-out scenario. The Swede leaps across into the driver's seat. Echoing the manoeuvre made by John Goodman's station wagon in *Raising Arizona*, Grimsrud turns the car a hundred and eighty degrees, fishtailing wildly, and puts pedal to metal. If we didn't already know how serious the situation is, Grimsrud taking a last drag on his cigarette and flicking it out of the window proves it. It takes a lot for the man to be parted from his Marlboro.

After a short pursuit, there's a screech of tyres and the tail lights of the couple's car vanish. Slowing down the

Ciera, Grimsrud spots them, in a pool of red light down an embankment at the roadside. The car has flipped, its wheels still spinning. The driver, an easy target in his red coat, makes a run for it across the snow. A single pistol shot to the back brings him down. Grimsrud finds his abandoned female companion trapped upside-down in the wreckage. No mercy. Another fatal shot rings out across the plains.

We don't see Showalter's reaction, but we can guess how the encounter looked to him, stranded back up the road half a mile away, with the DNA of the state trooper leaking all over him: the disappearing rear lights of the Ciera, the descending roar of its engine, the gunshots echoing their way back to him on the still air.

And let's definitely consider what's just happened from Jean's perspective – too often an ignored viewpoint. We've not seen her face since she disappeared behind that shower curtain; shortly after that, she was plunged into the darkness of the sack over her head.

Being hooded means she at least didn't get to witness the brutality of what's just occurred. She did, though, hear all three killings. The grunt of the state trooper, the moan of the other driver, the trio of gunshots. If she didn't fear for her life before, Jean must now strongly believe that it's odds-on she'll come to a premature end.

Between being snatched at home earlier that day and now being present at three murders, in contemplative moments in the trunk or on the back seat, Jean will have been wondering just who made her the centre of an abduction. Obviously, the ransom demand will be asked of her father. Has the whole scheme been dreamed up by someone wronged by business dealings with Wade, someone familiar with the Gustafson Growl? Jean wouldn't have a clue that the perpetrator was her husband, her hon. Nor will she ever.

Jerry Lundegaard's simple plan, constructed during quiet moments in that office at Gustafson Motors and seeming to be perfectly plausible in the cold light of day, now runs red with blood. It'll need someone with a sharp brain and a fearless resolve to mop it all up.

FOURTEEN

'I'LL FIX YA SOME EGGS'

It's about time we met our hero.

There's not yet been a single character to champion, no one to root for. We've already been presented with enough evidence to convince us that Jerry is a figure of antipathy. His charge sheet is already lengthy – misleading his customers, having his wife kidnapped, defrauding his father-in-law – and it will lengthen further. We won't be siding with his father-in-law anytime soon either, despite his being the target of the conspiracy and probably deserving some of our sympathy since his daughter has just been kidnapped. But unless his character performs a U-turn as dramatic as the one Grimsrud just pulled in pursuit of those witnesses on that highway, Wade's belligerence and pugnacity don't mark him out as hero material. We'll have to look elsewhere.

Of course, that 'elsewhere' doesn't include any place that Showalter and Grimsrud leave a boot print in the snow or a dripping trail of blood. The former's general toxicity and the latter's dead-eyed ruthlessness mean we're already collectively rooting for their comeuppance. Those crimes against the innocent must be punished by justice, whether custodial or by means more grave. It's just uncertain who's going to mete that justice out. Now, thirty minutes into the film, that person is about to make their belated, undramatic entrance.

As the sound of the gunshot that took care of the second witness fades on the night air, the film moves inside, out of the cold. It's a change of pace and tone. The camera slowly pans across a painting of a Canada goose, accompanied by the soft sound of that fiddle reprising the score's main theme. It's there to soothe us, to reassure us that, after the chaos and carnage of the previous scene – soundtracked by the thump of timpani – the body count will stay steady for at least the next few minutes.

The camera continues to pan, revealing pots of paintbrushes upturned in jars, tubes of oil paint and a selection of artist's models. These aren't unclothed young women; they are taxidermied waterfowl. But then we get a surprise. This is no artist's studio. In the corner of the room is a double bed. In the darkness, a woman is sleeping soundly. It's unclear whether the gentle snoring is hers or that of the man whose bald head is partly visible beyond her. As the camera moves in close, the phone rings. Her eyes snap open in a split second. She answers before the phone rings a second time. There's clearly a duty here. There is no option to ignore it, to carry on sleeping.

'Hi, it's Marge,' she whispers.

The man alongside her grunts and loops a heavy arm around her. The phone has disturbed him, but still she whispers.

'Oh, my. Where? . . . Yah . . . Oh, geez . . . Okay, there in a jiff . . . Real good, then.' That she needs to be there in a jiff suggests nothing remotely 'real good' has occurred.

Just as she has a duty to get up now, so too does the man in the bed (she's wearing a band of gold, so we can assume that he is Marge's husband). 'I'll fix ya some eggs,' he says. He might be on sleepy autopilot, but he knows this is his role. He repeats the line twice more, as much to instruct his sleep-addled brain what to do as to reassure his wife. This may well be a routine that's played out before. Perhaps several times before. And in the simple act of making some breakfast, we see more humanity, more kindness, than has been witnessed in the half-hour since the opening titles. These are the good guys. That's clear.

If Marge is to be our hero, she's an unlikely one, in her full-length, full-sleeve nightdress and with a makeshift artist's studio in the corner of her bedroom. When she rises from the bed, an extra dimension suggests she's not the obvious saviour. She is heavily pregnant.

As the action – if such sleepy, snail-slow movement can truly be called 'action' – moves downstairs into the kitchen-diner, confirmation arrives that Marge has indeed been cast in the role of hero, of saviour, of warrior for justice. Her husband (by now we know he answers to 'Norm') has managed to wrap a dressing gown around his big frame, but she's now dressed for work, despite it not yet being sunrise. And those clothes reveal the part she will play in the rest of the film: they are those of a police officer. The star attached to her shirt shows her seniority. This is why she's been woken in the early hours.

The scene's easy choreography is further confirmation that the situation is not an unfamiliar one to the couple, that they're no strangers to their sleep being interrupted by a ringing telephone. For starters, Norm hasn't bothered to make any breakfast for himself. He knows that Marge will head out before finishing hers and that he can simply drag the plate across the table and polish off the remains of the egg and the ham and the toast. Indeed, he doesn't even ask what the nature of the call is, what accident or crime or misdemeanour has occurred that needs her immediate action.

Marge's departure is far from immediate, though. Her protestations towards Norm's insistence on cooking up some sustenance ('You gotta eat a breakfast') were far from convincing. She then discovers that her police car, her prowler, has a flat battery and will need a jump-start. This isn't exactly rapid response. It's the first indication that the area of her jurisdiction might not be a high-crime area.

This scene, Marge and Norm's first, is as intimate and homely as their house. And the house is significant. As shown by the cramped kitchen-diner, it's nowhere near as large as the Lundegaards' home down in the Minneapolis suburbs, but they are clearly a happier, better-matched (and obviously more loving) couple despite this. That the art studio – later revealed to be the source of Norm's income – occupies the bedroom is further proof of their modest environment. Perhaps Norm has had to move his canvasses and paints and stuffed birds out of the spare room to convert it into a nursery in time for the imminent arrival. Perhaps he's even painted some birds on the nursery walls, ready for Junior to be able to tell a mallard from a common loon.

Within just two minutes spent inside Marge and Norm's tiny home (what estate agents would undoubtedly spin as 'cosy'), the Coens have introduced what's arguably the film's overarching theme: the battle of modest domesticity versus greedy ambition. This is a couple who, certainly at this early stage, are seemingly comfortable with the limits of their lives. Sure, they'll have dreams like everybody else, but they won't resort to devious, immoral means to realise them. Norm isn't the kind of man to have his wife kidnapped. He makes her breakfast instead. We suspect he's never had a cruel intention in his life.

Over the remaining hour of the film, though, it's up to Marge to unpick the cruel intentions of others. The moral weight of the film rests upon her shoulders. Will she deliver us from evil?

FIFTEEN

'THIS EXECUTION-TYPE DEAL'

Nonchalant. Insular. Inexperienced. Bumbling. Corrupt. Lazy. Out of their depth. Plain dumb.

Hollywood hasn't treated small-town cops very well. From the Deep South of *Live and Let Die* to the West Country of *Hot Fuzz* and many points in between, the movie industry has shown scant respect for police officers whose jurisdiction lies out in the middle of nowhere. Indeed, the more remote the small town, the more nonchalant/insular/inexperienced/bumbling/corrupt/ lazy/out of their depth/plain dumb their portrayal. These are the limits that Hollywood has largely set itself in this regard. If they're not a wrong 'un themselves, at best a rural police officer will be the character offering some light relief. They're rarely heroic figures.

When it comes to introducing the audience to the crack detectives who'll be charged with solving these murders outside Brainerd and bringing the miscreants to justice, it appears that the Coens are revisiting that cinematic trope, retreading the same territory as their fellow film-makers. First, there was the leisurely, unhurried way that the leader of these crack detectives – Marge Gunderson – left home for the crime scene: the breakfast, the flat battery. There was no sense that she's in charge of an emergency service, primed and ready to serve. There was no rush, no panic. Those cadavers aren't going anywhere, after all; though someone should tell her, in her sleepy state, that the killers are. They're distancing themselves from the scene with every delayed minute.

The darkness may have lifted by the time Marge arrives on the slushy highway to cast an eye over the night's horrors, but it's replaced by a blanket of grey gloom. A blue sky wouldn't suit the scene. She's greeted by a colleague, Lou, who didn't seem to be in a special hurry to get there either. He stopped off for coffee on the way for himself and his boss. And then there's the tone of Marge's voice, which is far from sombre. 'Whoooo! What ya got there?' she calls out as the coffee is handed across. 'So, what's the deal now? Gary says triple homicide.'

Both officers show a casualness, almost a nonchalance,

that suggests finding three murder victims dumped by the roadside is an everyday occurrence around these parts, that constantly dealing with bloodied bodies is an occupational hazard. Clue: it isn't. For a low-crime town like Brainerd, this would be a once-in-a-generation incident. And yet Marge isn't flustered, or shocked, or overwhelmed. She might as well be attending a minor car accident, a slight fender bender at a crosstown junction.

Lou is similarly laid-back. 'It looks pretty bad,' he announces in his sing-song accent, arguably the most sing-song of all *Fargo*'s characters. No shit, Lou. Don't go overselling it now. Best not get too melodramatic.

At this point, it's as if the Coens want us to believe that these two representatives of the local police department are out of their depth, that they haven't truly absorbed the brutality of the crimes they're about to investigate. With the deep snow nearly causing Marge to take a tumble as she approaches the upside-down car, we're led to believe that, should these crimes get solved by this bumbling pair, it'll be down to luck over judgement.

Then comes the kicker. Despite all the evidence she's presented about herself thus far, this police chief is no bumbler. Marge's brain has been working quickly. She only arrived on the crime scene a minute earlier, but she's already nailed the chronology of events.

'Okay, so we got a trooper pulls someone over, we got a shooting, and these folks drive by, and we got a high-speed pursuit, ends here, and this execution-type deal.'

This is why there's a star on her uniform.

'Yah,' says Lou, as if he'd already unpicked the sequence of events himself. Lou says 'yah' a lot.

'I'd be very surprised if our suspect's from Brainerd,' concludes Marge.

As well as being shown the sharpness of her detective's brain, we're also given an early measure of the stoicism that Marge will display for the rest of the film when she crouches down next to the victims' car and says, 'I think I'm gonna barf.' That it's a brief wave of morning sickness causing the nausea, rather than the sight of the aftermath of a young woman's gruesome, point-blank execution, tells us Marge Gunderson is made of strong stuff.

The pair relocate to examine the body of the state trooper, dumped in a ditch further up the highway. Again, Marge's investigative instinct comes to the fore. She's already sussed out the narrative; now it's a case of working out the *dramatis personae*.

The answer is in the snow. Well, if not the answer, then a big clue. Having spied the size of Grimsrud's boot prints earlier and concluded he's 'a big fella', Marge spots a different set next to the trooper. 'Yah, this guy's smaller than his buddy,' she calls to Lou. The simplicity of her investigative powers has yielded immediate results. No team of forensic scientists patiently combing the tundra for clues could have produced such a plausible overview in an entire day's worth of investigation. Gut and instinct, gut and instinct.

Not only does Marge know the crimes committed, the manner in which they were carried out and that the two victims back down the road were innocent bystanders, she also now knows that the search will be for two perpetrators rather than a lone gunman. And she knows that one is big and the other is small. An odd couple.

It's an impressive couple of minutes of detective work, a calm, methodical joining of the dots. There are hidden depths to this woman, despite outward appearances and first impressions. Or, as Frances McDormand declared to talk-show host Charlie Rose, 'she's extremely simple to figure out. There's not much complicated about Marge. But she's still surprising.'

We like surprises and we're on her side immediately. Among this bunch of characters of dubious motivations and villainous deeds, Marge is on the right side of the story. Just as the *Los Angeles Times* said of McDormand's performance in *Mississippi Burning* eight years earlier, she is 'the film's sole voice of morality'.

Major crimes of this nature might not come across her desk too frequently here in the backwoods, but when they do, this is one police chief who's ready for the challenge, whose intellect and instinct have already begun to unpick the tangle of events.

Sadly, we can't say the same about Lou.

Marge's deputy doesn't subvert the trope of the simple, slow-witted local cop. There are no hidden depths here. He doesn't surprise us. In fact, he doesn't do much at all.

At both crime scenes, he's perfectly happy to keep his distance from the bodies. He stays on the shoulder of the highway, merely an observer as his seven-months-pregnant chief heads into snow-filled ditches, bending and crouching as she examines the human wreckage. Lou merely holds the coffees, calling across with the odd 'How's it look, Margie?'.

A generous appraisal of his inaction would be that he is simply deferring to authority, respectful of the strata of seniority. Another thought is that while Brainerd's crime rate remains low and the crimes themselves minor, he's perfectly capable of appearing competent. But when a serious demeanour needs investigating, he's not got the wit or brains to step up. Remaining on the highway, away from the gore, suggests he might be a tad squeamish too. When gun-toting hoodlums start shooting up the locals, Lou is left wanting. At that point, his greatest contribution involves bringing a hot beverage to his boss.

Marge is well aware of this. She doesn't use Lou as a sounding board; she knows he's not the world's deepest thinker. He's not one to be consulted when it comes to cracking a tricky case, to unpicking crime scenes and weaving them into a plausible, motive-strengthened narrative. Instead, Marge uses him more as an echo chamber. When audibly chewing over events, she's effectively just thinking out loud. Lou's opinion isn't really being courted (he's rarely in possession of one, after all), but the inevitable 'Yah' that comes back in Marge's direction does, in a strange way, help to confirm and crystallise her thinking.

It's not a flowing, two-way exchange between equals. It's more minimalist than that, prompting one reviewer to remark that 'it hadn't previously occurred to me that the ranks of American law enforcement could be swelled by importing *dramatis personae* from the work of Samuel Beckett'.

They head back into town. Marge has shown her undeniable detective chops out there on the highway – the skills that have helped her climb through the ranks to the top job. Lou, on the other hand, has demonstrated that her ascent may not have been all that difficult. If the other applicants for the post of police chief were of a similar calibre to him, Marge would have been a shoo-in.

Indeed, Marge is still having to steer Lou's investigative work as if he were a novice cop and not the middle-aged officer with a decade or two's experience behind him. When she asks if there are any clues about the assailants in the trooper's citation book, Lou proudly announces that he's got police across the state looking for a car with a licence plate beginning DLR, having figured out that they stopped him before he could finish writing down the tag number.

Marge knows to pay close attention to any sentence Lou utters that begins with 'I figured . . .'. And her put-down – containing one of the most quoted lines of the whole film – is both charitable and diplomatic.

'I'm not sure I agree with you a hunnert percent on your policework there, Lou.'

'Yah?'

'Yah. I think that vehicle there probably had dealer plates. DLR?'

Lou looks crestfallen. His biggest contribution thus far to catching the perpetrators of the most major crime to hit Brainerd and its immediate environs in years has been rendered useless. His balloon has been popped. He feels a fool. Even more of a fool than normal.

'Oh . . .'

A beat. The cogs turn.

'Geez . . .'

SIXTEEN

EMBERS

When he wrote the introduction to the published screenplay, one particular line of Ethan Coen's hit the mark with all the precision of Gaear Grimsrud gunning down a fleeing witness. He unsentimentally describes his home state as 'a bleak, windswept tundra, resembling Siberia except for its Ford dealerships and Hardee's restaurants'.

In this statement, Coen made a concession to a national, and international, readership. Hardee's is the most recognisable name when it comes to family restaurants in the US, a chain boasting several thousand establishments across the country. It was a reference that most would recognise; they would have got the point Ethan was making. He almost certainly would have preferred to mention Embers, the Minnesota-based chain with restaurants dotted around the Twin Cities and further afield. But few beyond the state line would have got the reference. Still, no matter. The Coens instead paid their homage to the chain by setting a scene in its St Louis Park branch, a doughnut's throw from the busy I-394 highway. It's where, over coffee, Jerry, Wade and Stan discuss the tactics of how to pay the ransom: specifically, how *much* to pay.

The diner is a staple of American cinema – from *True Romance* to *American Graffiti*, *Goodfellas* to *Five Easy Pieces*, *Back to the Future* to, er, *Diner*. Originally, it was the crucible for youthful exuberance and mild rebellion in 1950s-set films, the place where the decade's teens could loosen up away from the suffocating ways of their starchy parents. Its customers wore varsity jackets and quiffs. They sipped milkshakes and enthusiastically fed dimes into the jukebox. An obligatory wide-finned car would be idling out front, the chariot of misadventure.

Later, the diner grew to resemble something more sinister; it became the meeting place of choice for Hollywood's more criminally inclined fraternity. In its booths, heists were planned and executions commissioned. Sometimes, the diner was the crime scene itself: see Mickey and Mallory's killing spree in the opening scene of *Natural*

Born Killers, or lovebirds Pumpkin and Honey Bunny holding up the entire joint in *Pulp Fiction*.

To the film-maker, the diner offers plenty. A booth is an intimate, enclosed space where a scene is often reduced to the barest of its bare essentials: the dialogue. It also has the benefit of placing the protagonists on neutral ground, stripped of the advantage of home turf. We can see who they really are, how they really behave, whether they deserve our favour.

In purely culinary terms, Embers makes for a fine rendezvous. Almost every craving is catered for within its voluminous eight-page menu. The chain was founded by two school pals in 1956, four years before Hardee's opened their first restaurant, and, at its height, had several dozen branches. It was a Minnesotan institution.

Fargo's ransom-discussing party make their visit during daytime hours, but Embers – or, at least, the branch I regularly frequented – was at its most alluring during the wee small hours when the rest of the city slept. Here, primarily attracted by the $3.99 steak and eggs special, a rich and varied collection of nighthawks would populate its booths. Drunks who'd been turned out of bars and needed a bite to eat to soak up the liquor swilling around inside them. Blue-collar workers fuelling up before their shifts started at first light. College students taking a break from trying to complete an assignment due on their professor's desk in the morning. Clandestine lovers seeking out the darkest, most discreet corner booths.

And police officers. Always police officers. I can't remember a time when the Minneapolis PD weren't represented in at least one or two of its booths, taking advantage of those endless coffee refills that would see them through a night of crime-fighting. Once, at around three in the morning, an officer took me and a couple of pals out front to admire his squad car's firepower. Not the size of the engine under the hood. The collection of shotguns stowed in the trunk.

Jerry Lundegaard is fortunate that, on the trio's visit to Embers, no member of the Minneapolis PD is taking refreshment. If they were, Wade would have been straight across to their table to secure their assistance. As it is, his son-in-law is doing all he can to dissuade him from simply picking up the phone and involving the authorities.

'All's I know is, ya got a problem, ya call a professional!' protests Wade.

'No! They said no cops! They were darned clear on that, Wade! They said you call your cops and we gonna shoot –'

The neutral ground of the diner certainly helps Jerry's cause, allowing him to keep his plan on course. The last time the three met was in Wade's office. This time, he isn't forced to perch on the arm of a chair. He's seated in the middle of the trio and, uncharacteristically empowered, appears to have the upper hand in the direction of the discussion. Against all odds, he's gone from humdrum everyman to forceful negotiator. And, in a rare moment of dissension from his boss, even Stan, the loyal lieutenant, believes getting the police involved is too risky. 'I gotta tell you, Wade, I'm leanin' to Jerry's viewpoint here.'

This makes Wade growl louder than ever.

This is the only time we'll see Jerry get his way over that of his father-in-law. Wade treats the ransom request as if it were a business deal, as if securing Jean's release was comparable to the haggling and hammering-out of a corporate takeover. He's shielding a reputation for never giving anyone exactly what they want, a *modus operandi* he's keen to uphold. It's of little significance that the safety and security of his daughter is at stake. Accordingly, Wade moots the idea of offering the kidnappers half a million, half of what they are demanding. Or, at least, half of what Jerry claims they are demanding. Stan again applies the brakes, explaining that they're not horse-trading here. 'We just gotta bite the bullet on this thing.'

Of course, the real pivotal moment of this scene isn't the victory Jerry scores over Wade. It's the revelation that his evilness reaches much deeper than we previously believed. The actual ransom is more than ten times what we understood it to be. He's fleecing the old guy for a seven-figure amount, while also double-crossing the kidnappers, only paying them $40,000, along with the Ciera freshly liberated from Wade's showroom. It's a grand scheme for sure, an audacious conspiracy – and all revealed in the humble surroundings of a low-budget restaurant. It's only fair that Jerry picks up the tab for the coffee.

Today, if you fancied sitting at the same table, on the same vinyl seating, as these three, you'd be out of luck. Only a single Embers restaurant remains in existence, and it's not the one in St Louis Park. Coffee is no longer served on that site, nor pancakes, nor steak and egg specials. The building has undergone a radical change of purpose. The only visitors to 7525 Wayzata Boulevard these days are patients travelling there to undergo their latest bout of kidney dialysis.

The insomniacs of Embers are ghosts now. As is a certain mid-1970s teenager, with glasses and a giant bulb of curly hair, who once washed dishes out the back, here in the St Louis Park branch. Twenty-odd years later, Ethan Coen returned to the site of his first job with a film crew in tow.

Again, everything gets used.

SEVENTEEN

WHO'S GOT THE BEST COAT?

I thought I was ready for my first Minnesotan winter. It turned out I wasn't.

When the first chill winds blew down from the north in early November, I paid a visit to a second-hand clothes store in the Dinkytown neighbourhood, on the far side of the University of Minnesota campus. These days, it would probably market itself as a vintage store, with price tags several times higher than those that adorned the clothing when originally sold. Back then, though, it was still very much a thrift store, with a pricing scheme agreeable to the tightest of budgets.

In its deepest, darkest recesses, I pulled out a light-shaded sheepskin coat with cream-coloured faux-fur lining and lapels. It fitted like a dream. More importantly, it was just six dollars. I strutted up and down in front of a mirror as I considered its suitability. I fancied myself as Bob Dylan on the cover of *Freewheelin'*, ambling down the middle of a city street with a hopelessly devoted girlfriend on my arm. That prompted another consideration. Dylan had honed his art and debuted his early songs in the coffee-houses of these very Dinkytown streets. Not only that, but the apartment he lived in – above Gray's Drugstore – was just three doors down from this second-hand clothing emporium. Could it be, could it really be, that this actual coat used to be a fixture of the Dylan wardrobe? Maybe he was even wearing it, in the austere chill of his apartment, when he made the seismic decision to switch from being plain old Robert Zimmerman to icon-in-waiting Bob Dylan. I was sold. I handed over the cash and wore the coat out onto the street, strutting past the window of his old apartment.

That coat would be my first choice of outerwear that entire winter despite all its limitations and inadequacies. It was fine for trips downtown, where the combination of frequent buses and the Skyway system meant you weren't exposed to the elements for too long. And it kept you just about warm enough if you were in a lengthy queue at Minneapolis nightspot First Avenue to see one of the city's better bands. Once over the threshold, I would recklessly undo a couple of the coat's brass buttons. But I'd never take it off and hand it over to the cloakroom attendant. It could have been Bob Dylan's old coat, after all. It was staying on my shoulders.

Beyond the Twin Cities, though, this coat was woefully lacking in weather-beating properties. I'd only owned it about three weeks before I realised this, while on a Thanksgiving Weekend road trip up to Duluth on the shores of Lake Superior. With the town effectively in shutdown, thus leaving ill-prepared visitors at the mercy of the unforgiving elements, I was cut in two by the ferocity of the wind coming off the lake. I've still never been anywhere colder in my life. Duluth is a place where even hardened polar explorers would do their zipper right up. It was also another staging post in the life of the young Dylan, so when he later wrote the line 'The wind howls like a hammer', I'm pretty sure I know the exact source of his inspiration.

In the new year, when the heavy snows of January and February landed in Minneapolis, this prized coat of mine proved even more unsuitable. The snow simply soaked right through, drenching the layers underneath. If caught in a snowstorm, it would take days to dry out.

Carl Showalter was another out-of-towner who plumped for a sheepskin coat. His was quite similar to mine, albeit in a milk-chocolate shade, with faux-fur lapels of a similar hue. But it didn't make him look as cool as the young Bob Dylan either – not even when offset by a turtleneck sweater underneath. In fact, *definitely* not when offset by a turtleneck sweater underneath.

If we extend the theory that Showalter is actually Mr Pink from *Reservoir Dogs*, his innocence when it comes to the most appropriate outerwear for these extreme temperatures is understandable. It may well be the transplanted Californian's first experience of a Minnesotan winter.

His partner Grimsrud has no such excuses. While he admits it's the first time he's been to Minneapolis, the sub-zero temperatures of his native Scandinavia should have prepared him well. Instead, though, he's opted for a wholly inappropriate leather coat to ward off the cold, one that's practically wafer-thin compared to the protection and plump of the more popular padded jacket. (Grimsrud's one sartorial concession to the cold is the wearing of long johns. However, at the remote cabin – where the temperatures

will be significantly lower than those of the Twin Cities –
he opts to wear them without trousers over the top. Silly
boy. He'll catch his death.)

As expected, it's the locals who know the right winterwear
to cocoon themselves from those months of severe weather.
It's all about insulation. 'Everyone is bulked up,' observes
Joel Coen, 'moving in a particular way, bouncing off
people. That sponginess is part of the regional flavour.'

But who carries it off the best?

For the lifelong residents of Minnesota, and certainly for
the main characters in *Fargo*, the parka is indeed the coat of
choice. It's windproof, it's waterproof and it's warm, warm,
warm. Jerry, of course, opts for one in bland beige. Stan's
is a comparatively brave deep red, almost a crimson, with
royal blue detail and lining.

Wade is another champion of the faithful parka (his is
an attractive pea-green effort), but he'll discover to his cost
the limits of its protective qualities. It turns out that it's
not all-conquering. It can't repel gunfire. When Showalter
empties his handgun into Wade's midriff, the coat's lining
explodes in a little puff, like a snowball making contact
with its target.

Both Stan and Wade are attired just the same as the local entrepreneurs who Joel Coen approached when he was trying to drum up finance for *Blood Simple*. 'I remember having meetings with these hardened businessmen,' he later recalled, 'who would hang out in the local coffee shop and then put their parkas and galoshes on and slog out into this Siberian landscape.'

But the best coat in the film belongs to Marge. It's a standard-issue Brainerd PD garment that puts functionality over fashion. Chunky but still sufficiently generous in its proportions to fit comfortably over a seven-months-pregnant belly, it boasts the twin security of both zipper and poppers, as well as a fur-lined snorkel hood. And, of course, Marge's comes with a shiny gold star pinned to the left breast.

This is a coat made for keeping its wearer warm and dry when examining the bodies of murder victims on snowbound, sub-zero highways. You never see Marge shiver in a fierce wind. You never see her clothes damp from snowfall that's penetrated her outer layer.

Now *that's* the coat I should have bought from the second-hand store.

EIGHTEEN

MINNESOTA NICE

When I lived in Minneapolis, there were a couple of grocery stores on the main drag that ran through my neighbourhood. One was an anonymous branch of an anonymous chain. The other, which got the majority of my custom, was a smaller independent store where the service was much more personal. And whether I crossed its threshold at seven in the morning or ten at night, the same bespectacled, middle-aged woman would be sitting next to the cash register just inside the door. (I remember her name to be Rosie, but this might just be down to the complexion of her cheeks, or the fact that I bought a shiny red apple from her store every day.)

As I was a regular customer, and as she seemed to be the only person working there whatever the hour, we would have the usual daily conversations about sport, snowfall or soda brands. Rosie was one of the first people – and one of the friendliest – I met during my time in the city. Ours was the kind of easy, unforced interaction that you would expect to find in some outlying small town rather than the centre of a major metropolis. Not that it was layered, nuanced discourse. Nor did it touch on personal matters. It was little more than chit-chat, but it helped to humanise urban living. Rosie had a habit of ending every other sentence with 'You betcha'. This seemed eminently open and friendly. I soon realised that most other people in the neighbourhood – the waitresses at my usual bar, the pizza-delivery boy – were equally outgoing. They too liberally littered their conversation with 'You betcha'.

This was my introduction to the concept of Minnesota Nice, a state of outward pleasantness that, over time, has been considered a state-specific characteristic. Not that it's a concept easily constrained by a simple definition. It runs deeper than merely describing the bonhomie of service-industry employees. It's more amorphous and intangible.

Rachel Hutton, a columnist with the *Star Tribune*, the state's biggest daily newspaper, has attempted to corral the concept. She believes it to be 'Minnesotans' tendency to be polite and friendly, yet emotionally reserved; our penchant for self-deprecation and unwillingness to draw attention to ourselves; and, most controversially, our maddening habit of substituting passive-aggressiveness for direct confrontation'.

To the team behind the nationally syndicated radio show *A Prairie Home Companion*, the concept took the form of Wobegonics: a way of verbal interaction that contains 'no confrontational verbs or statements of strong personal preference'. Some have noted its occasionally superficial nature – that it obscures true feelings and intentions. As R. T. Rybak, a former three-term mayor of Minneapolis, half-jokingly observed, 'Minnesotans will give you directions to anywhere but their house.'

There's a well-attended school of thought that believes Minnesota Nice to have its roots in the state's Scandinavian heritage. The 1933 novel *A Fugitive Covers His Tracks*, by the Norwegian writer Aksel Sandemose, set out a ten-point doctrine called the Law of Jante. Although a satirical literary creation, the law's 'rules' had a strong cultural impact in Scandinavia, reflecting – and promoting – attitudes across the region when it came to conforming, to not standing out, to not doing something extreme or too ambitious.

For instance, the first rule determined that 'You're not to think you're anything special'. This exactly mirrors Ethan's portrait of Marge, as described to the film critic Nigel Floyd. 'Minnesota people are sort of down-to-earth. One never presents oneself as a big shot in that kind of culture. So Marge doesn't hold herself up as anything extraordinary. It's just how she is.'

The Law of Jante declared that the preservation of society's stability and uniformity was king. And it's believed that the law's influence, bequeathed through the bloodlines of migrating Scandinavians, came to flavour the cultural characteristics – modest, non-confrontational – of a state where a third of the population has Viking heritage. Their ancestors were the hardiest of immigrants. They pushed on, further into the interior, further into the tundra, further into the void.

I just found the little red address book I was using when I lived in Minnesota. In it are the names of people I've long since forgotten. Most of the names are of north European origin, and most of these are Scandinavian or German. And here's the thing. Almost all the folk with either Swedish or Norwegian names (Olson, Anderson, several

Carlsons, there's even a Gustafson) are from Minnesota. And almost everyone with Germanic surnames (Schmidt, Gehring, Maierhofer) are from Wisconsin, the state to the immediate east. Now, I'm no ethnographer, but this small sample – admittedly from thirty-odd years ago – suggests two things to me. One, that the flaxen-headed Vikings did indeed push on further, while the Germans were content to put down sturdy roots in Wisconsin; and, two, that social mobility is low-priority up here in the northern states. The apples stay close to the tree.

The Scandinavian influence is certainly still very conspicuous across Minnesota. Swedish churches and restaurants dot the map. 'It's more Sweden than Sweden,' observed *Fargo*'s one true Scandi, Peter Stormare. 'There's no town in Sweden that has portraits of the king and queen in a shop window or in the diner.'

This transplanted sense of uniformity plays a vital role throughout the film. It provides the neutral backdrop to the outlandish, extraordinary events that will take place on its plains and at its parking lots and in its wood chippers. It heightens the shock value, making the violence more visceral and the scarlet bloodshed more vivid. As Ethan

Coen has noted, it's all about 'the conflict between that constant avoidance of all confrontation and the murders gradually piling up'.

Whatever the source, there are liberal examples of Minnesota Nice throughout the film: Jean's nervous, subservient behaviour when her father's around for supper; the wife of Jerry's irate customer attempting to pacify her angry husband lest he make too public a show of them; Marge's congenial interview technique when questioning dangerous former cons like Shep Proudfoot: 'So you think you might remember who those folks were who called ya?'

Indeed, so ingrained is that sense of public politeness that Marge will take far more offence at Jerry's rudeness towards her than she does at the brutality of the murders committed on her patch.

(Wade, however, is no subscriber to the concept of Minnesota Nice. He's the polar opposite. Being outwardly friendly and considerate to others doesn't wash in the boardroom. He didn't get where he is by not rocking apple carts. He upturned them. This is a man who loves a confrontation. Thrives on it, in fact. There's an element of conflict in every single scene in which he appears.)

The main proponent of Minnesota Nice is surely his son-in-law. For starters, Jerry's profession – one that requires a geniality that's at least surface-deep – is perfect for its cultivation. A car salesman only has to set a tone. He doesn't need to go deep, discussing Hegelian dialectics or Newton's third law of motion with his clients. Keep on safe territory. Platitudes, painted smiles, smooth talking. That'll do it.

But so entrenched within Jerry's psyche is this *modus operandi* that he uses it throughout his wider life, even when there's far more at stake than persuading a customer to sign up to a financing deal. Take the Embers scene, for instance. With Wade having stormed out of the diner, frustrated by his impotency surrounding the ransom (and, almost certainly, by the otherwise faithful Stan opposing his suggestion of calling in the cops or offering a lower ransom payment), Jerry heads to the cash register to settle the bill.

'How was everything today?' asks the chirpy cashier.

'Yah, real good now.'

The veneer Jerry deploys here covers all aspects of his life. Everything is a half-lie – at the very minimum. His truthful answer to the cashier should be: 'My world is collapsing. It's a disaster. I'm up to my neck in debt. I've had my wife kidnapped, but my overbearing patriarch of a father-in-law is hijacking the plan. I'm on the brink of a chronic existential crisis. It's dark, dark, dark.' Instead, appearances have to be kept up – even though the other diners would surely have turned their heads at the heated exchanges between the three, not to mention at Wade stomping out the door.

'Real good' is Jerry's most common verbal tic (although 'The heck d'ya mean?' and 'You're darn tootin'' both run it close). It's a comfort blanket for him, one he wraps himself in regardless of the gravity of the situation. It's his answer to Jean when she innocuously asks him how the trip to Fargo was. It's his way of keeping his equilibrium when the demands of Reilly Diefenbach from GMAC pull the noose tighter. And, most extraordinarily of all, it's his sign-off to a call from a desperate Showalter who's just threatened to exterminate his family.

'. . . I shoot you, and I shoot your fucking wife, and I shoot all your little fucking children, and I shoot 'em all in the back of their little fucking heads. You got it? GOT IT?!'

'Okay, real good, then.'

NINETEEN

THE DEMEANING OF JEAN

No one fares worse in *Fargo* than Jean Lundegaard. She has the raw end of every deal.

The best we see of her is in the last moments of peace she'll ever experience. On her own with time to herself: just her, her knitting and some amiable daytime television. It's pretty much the only time we see her smile. And then Carl Showalter comes stomping up her back steps to shatter the peace – and the nearest windowpane.

When Jean disappears into the folds and creases of the shower curtain, we never see her face again – aside from Marge glancing at her photo in Jerry's office. From car trunk to cabin floor, that sack will never come off her head. She's in the dark for the rest of her life: literally and metaphorically. She doesn't know who these men are. She doesn't know what they want with her. But she does know, from the violent way they took her from the sanctuary of her suburban home, just how dangerous they can be. The events out on the highway after dark simply confirm this.

When the Ciera arrives at the cabin hideaway the next morning, Showalter appears to have shrugged off any trauma from the bloody deeds of a few hours earlier. Pulling Jean out of the car, he allows her to blindly attempt to escape, her bare feet taking her in all directions on the crinkled crunch of virgin snow. She's stumbling and tumbling, and his laughter fills the dead air. 'Whoops!' he cackles. Zero thoughts are given to the distress that hearing three brutal executions would have on her. Or the distress of whatever fate awaits her. For now, she's a figure of fun.

Not only is Jean hooded, but her hands are bound and she's tied to a chair for the entire time she's in the cabin. She's gagged throughout too. With her face hidden from our view and her ability to speak removed, Jean becomes dehumanised. Faceless and silent, she's now just an object, a commodity, around which the entire deal, and the duplicitous double-double-crossing, pivot. She ceases to be a person. She might as well be a bag of diamonds or a stolen Old Master artwork.

Jean is the collateral damage of a simple plan that grows more complicated, more calamitous, at every turn. Showalter certainly seems to have forgotten that there's a human being under that sack. Later, on the one occasion that Jerry asks him about her welfare, the kidnapper seems a little confused.

'How's Jean?'

A pause that's longer than it should be.

'Who's Jean?'

While we're fractionally reassured that Jerry has remembered to enquire about his wife (albeit only after he learns that circumstances have changed 'beyond the, uh, acts of God, force majeure'), this is the only time we'll hear him voice any concern for Jean, at least beyond the plastic lines he'll spout to Wade just to keep the plan on track.

It's only in death that Jean will be delivered from the evil that's swallowed up nearly everyone in her orbit. And it's almost a blessing that she'll never know that it was the greed and callousness of her darling Jerry, her hon, that brought about her end.

TWENTY

WELCOME TO BRAINERD

Brainerd is an unremarkable town.

There's nothing wrong with that. That's exactly why the Coen brothers' metaphorical pin landed right on this part of the map, why they set such dastardly deeds here. Like the neutral tones of the Lundegaards' home or Wade's office, it's a blank canvas across which the plot can spread. No other distractions, no other interference. Across this quiet, low-level town, these extraordinary actions will stand out even more prominently. The extremes will seem more extreme. The events will be even more shocking.

Fargo fans aside, there's little reason why anyone would choose to visit the place. It was founded by the president of the Northern Pacific railroad, this being the point at which the Staples–Duluth railroad straddled the Mississippi River. Brainerd was his wife's maiden name. That visitor numbers to the town are low is confirmed by the fact that this is a railway town with no passenger trains serving it. The line is solely used for freight.

You get the sense that the odd freight train passing through, usually pulling a dozen or so coal wagons and with its horn emitting an extended, throaty wail, is among the highlights of any given day. The town couldn't be described as sleepy, but it's not exactly a hive of activity either. To the north of the railroad, there's a dual-lane highway that's identical to a thousand other dual-lane highways, lined with car lots, single-storey banks and the usual food offerings: Dairy Queen, McDonald's, Wendy's, Pizza Hut . . . The only difference with this familiar, could-be-anywhere picture is that it crosses the Mississippi.

On the other side of the tracks is Brainerd's older quarter. 'Welcome to Downtown Brainerd,' announces a cutesy wooden sign, 'A City For All Seasons. Since 1871.' Downtown is a bit of a misnomer. The area covers just a handful of blocks and there's barely a building more than two storeys high. There are a few more independent stores and restaurants here, but nothing that would properly put it on the tourist map, that would give someone a reason to visit. But, to its credit, it feels like a peaceful town, despite the tales that those mischievous Coen boys are telling about the place. Indeed, the last crime committed here that made the national headlines was when Baby Face Nelson held up the First National Bank of Brainerd in 1933.

Certainly, triple homicides of the like that Marge Gunderson is charged with investigating are low enough on the ground to be nonexistent. On East River Road, little more than a hundred metres from the banks of the Mississippi, sits the headquarters of the Brainerd Police Department, an undistinguished low-level building easily identified by the squad cars parked outside. When I visited, a couple of shaven-headed officers, untroubled by any pressing business, were leaning against their vehicles, chewing the fat. No triple homicides that day.

The police HQ is the first (and probably only) destination for *Fargo* fanboys and fangirls visiting Brainerd. The crew never set up their cameras here. Not a single second of the film was actually shot in the town; the only scene set in the police HQ was filmed in the now-demolished police station in Edina, back in the Minneapolis suburbs.

In *Fargo*, Brainerd is represented only by name. Those roads outside the town – where the monster statue of

Paul Bunyan stands menacingly on the verge, and where Grimsrud carries out those three shootings – aren't actually the roads outside the town. Those scenes were filmed three hundred miles to the north, outside Bathgate, North Dakota, a tiny settlement that has had city status conferred upon it, despite its population totalling forty-three individuals at the last count. The crew were forced to relocate there, just a few miles from the Canadian border, after one of Minnesota's mildest winters left too little snow on the ground further south.

Similarly, the Blue Ox scene was actually filmed back in the Twin Cities, at Stockman's truck stop in Saint Paul, an establishment that hasn't closed its doors even once since opening in 1954. Here, if you pump a hundred gallons or more of fuel into the tank of your rig, you earn yourself a free breakfast.

The population of Brainerd may well have felt aggrieved that no filming actually took place in their town, but their noses were certainly put out of joint when one or two (fictional) members of the local police force were portrayed as not being the sharpest tools in the shed. I imagine the Brainerd PD's officers themselves weren't overjoyed either.

Frank Ball was the town's chief of police when *Fargo* was released, but there was no danger of his being mistaken for pregnant Marge. Pictures of him at the time, showing him mugging in front of the sign on the city limits (Brainerd, POP. 12353) with his hand on his holstered gun, made him look like a crooked lawman in a David Lynch film. There was definitely a whiff of Willem Dafoe about him.

Even if it doesn't go overboard in celebrating it, over time Brainerd appears to have made peace with the film. When, in 2004, *Premiere* magazine named the hundred greatest movie characters of all time, Marge Gunderson came twenty-seventh. The local newspaper, the *Brainerd Dispatch*, noted with unconcealed pride how that put her 'one spot behind ET and three spots ahead of King Kong'.

TWENTY-ONE

GET YER 'YAH YAHS' OUT . . .

Lou has partially redeemed himself.

To redress the balance for his state-wide APB requesting that officers look for a tan Ciera with a licence plate beginning 'DLR', he's been hitting the phones, calling all hotels and motels in the area to see if they've recently been visited by anyone arriving in such a vehicle.

And he's hit paydirt. Two nights before, the Blue Ox – 'that truckers' joint out there on I-35' – received the patronage of two men registering a tan Ciera but failing to include the licence plate details. A great lead, as Marge acknowledges between dipping her lunchtime French fries into a swamp of ketchup. Some strong policework from Lou, for sure. But our favourite deputy has done even better. He's found out that the pair weren't discreet, under-the-radar guests. 'Owner was on the desk then, said these two had company.'

Marge catches up with the 'company' at a strip joint, the Lakeside Club, presumably where they work, and presumably where Showalter and Grimsrud picked them up before heading over to the Blue Ox. At the far end of the Lakeside Club's elevated dancing platform, she sits in front of the two young women who occupied the kidnappers' twin beds, first for sex and then for watching *The Tonight Show*. Maybe they even tried ordering room service for more of Grimsrud's beloved pancakes.

This is the scene in the whole film that's most played for laughs, with that Minnesota accent amplified more than ever for comedic effect. If we thought Lou was addicted to uttering 'Yah' at every comment or question aimed in his general direction, these two take it to another level. Marge's head bounces between them left and right as they bat yahs back at her.

It's clear who paired off with whom at the Blue Ox. The frizzy-haired first hooker – imaginatively named Hooker #1 in the screenplay and credits – is very talkative, but without actually saying too much. Over and over, she repeats how funny-looking Showalter was ('more'n most people even'). She is kinda funny-looking herself. They were a natural match. Hooker #2 is blonde and taller, just like her grunting bedmate Grimsrud.

Marge gains little information from the frizzy-haired one – certainly not enough to build up the slightest photo-fit in her head. She only learns that he wasn't circumcised, a nugget of information that couldn't be utilised in even the most curious of identity parades.

The blonde hooker gives nothing meaningful to Marge either. She paints a portrait of Grimsrud as looking like the Marlboro Man, but tempers this with the disclaimer that she might be remembering him that way simply because he smoked Marlboros – 'like a subconscious-type thing'.

But if Marge comes away from the strip club with no better description of the assailants she's pursuing, the chief has at least gained a minor lead. The trail hasn't gone completely cold.

Hooker #1: 'Hey, they said they were goin' to the Twin Cities.'

Marge nods. 'Oh, yah?'

Hooker #2: 'Yah.'

Hooker #1: 'Yah. Is that useful to ya?'

Marge, nodding her head some more: 'Oh, you betcha, yah.'

*

Hooker #1 was played by Larissa Kokernot. Aside from her unforgettably talkative turn, this Minneapolis native also operated as a voice coach on the *Fargo* set, helping the cast to skewer the accent handed down from Nordic and Swedish ancestry. And it needs to be skewered. Just like the meteorology of Minnesota, the state's accent is a *Fargo* character all of its own.

Kokernot advised Frances McDormand in particular on the ways of sounding like she was a native – perhaps surprising, with the latter being married to a certain Minnesotan by the name of Joel Coen. Kokernot showed McDormand how to deploy the correct body language whenever Marge is engaged in conversation, particularly when interviewing the two hookers. 'One thing I talked about with Frances was the whole Minnesota Nice notion of wanting people to agree with each other and get along. And that's where the whole head-nodding thing also comes in.'

Now a maths tutor in a middle school in north Minneapolis, Kokernot worked as an actor and theatre director for many years; *Fargo* remains the cinematic high point of her career. 'There was something about that movie – people focused in on that Minnesota sound. I do feel like it has that cachet now. I put it on my resumé as one of my dialects: Minnesotan.'

Michelle Hutchison, who played the escort later hired by Showalter, explained how *Fargo* was the first time that the accent 'was really put on the map in terms of something to be made fun of. And, of course, Minnesota people have a hard time laughing at themselves. A lot of people said, "Oh, we don't talk like that," but some of us do, and that's okay.' Indeed, *Fargo*'s cinematographer, the great Roger Deakins, initially thought that the actors playing the two truck-stop hookers were laying the accent on too thick, before realising that 'actually they spoke exactly like that'.

Others acknowledged that the Coens – in their meticulously scripted screenplay which, by including every last 'huh' and 'geez', left no room for improvisation – had amplified and exaggerated the local dialect, but were unhappy that this appeared to have been done largely for comic effect. The then mayor of Brainerd, Bonnie Cumberland (surely a name that belongs to a Coen brothers character), left the movie theatre unimpressed. 'I have a lot of "you betchas" in my vocabulary,' she admitted, 'but not that much.' Her citizens, she declared, shared her view. 'It's a movie that people who don't live here seem to enjoy, but for us it's a little bit of an embarrassment.'

This opinion went beyond Brainerd's city limits. Writing in *Time*, Richard Corliss snorted that the Coens had shown 'giddy contempt toward people who talk and think Minnesotan'. The *New Yorker's* reviewer was equally dismissive on the subject of the accent, observing that the characters 'deliver passionless conversation, as if their batteries were running low'. The man from the *New York Times* accused the brothers of being 'quislings' for portraying their fellow Minnesotans as 'slow-witted doofuses'.

'The people who are inclined to be offended will be,' was Ethan Coen's defence at the time. Certainly, rural Minnesotans had form when it came to being affronted by a portrayal of them; their noses had been knocked out of joint before. In 1920, the Minnesota-born novelist Sinclair

Lewis published his most famous work, the satire *Main Street*, which aimed its mild barbs at the petty-minded citizens of the fictional Minnesotan town of Gopher Prairie. Although the book played a large part in Lewis becoming the first American writer to be awarded the Nobel Prize for Literature ten years later, that success wasn't exactly met by an avalanche of applause back on home turf. Somewhat proving Lewis's point about small-town myopia, the public library of Alexandria, Minnesota, had already banned copies of *Main Street* from its shelves.

Aside from Kokernot and Hutchison, the Coens cast many other Minnesotans in *Fargo*'s support roles, actors who were already well-versed in the local dialect and tone. These included Melissa Peterman who, moving on from playing Hooker #2 in that Lakeside Club scene, became a successful comedy actor and TV host. Larry Brandenburg, who played Stan to the most perfect of notes, hails from the town of Wabasha, downriver from the Twin Cities. Despite being born and raised in Colorado, John Carroll Lynch (aka Norm) had worked for many years with the Guthrie Theater in Minneapolis, as did Bruce Bohne, the man behind perpetually confused Lou. The late Cliff

Rakerd, who played Lou's slightly-more-switched-on colleague Gary Olson, was a resident of Coon Rapids in the suburbs of north Minneapolis (where, incidentally, he served a local law firm as billing manager for thirty years; he was only a part-time actor). The Coens also recruited from just across the state line in North Dakota, only a mile or so, by plucking Fargo native Kristin Rudrüd to play Jean Lundegaard.

The Minnesotan accent – those flat As and forward Os – didn't come so naturally to *Fargo*'s out-of-state actors – the likes of McDormand, Macy and Harve Presnell. To assist them in getting the pitch correct and those vowel sounds spot-on, Ethan Coen gave interview tapes of northern Minnesotans to the film's official dialect coach, Elizabeth Himmelstein. Himmelstein, a native of Indiana, then spent two weeks in Minneapolis with the main actors ahead of the shoot to nail the accents. Not that everyone was completely on board, as she later recalled to Southern California Public Radio.

'What I wanted was for everybody to really commit to these accents, because it had so much to do with their characters. And so we went through every single sound and we drilled. At one point, Bill Macy said to me, "Thank you so much. This has been fantastic. I'm just going to do a subtle version and that's how I see it." I said, "That's fine with me." We were all living together in a hotel and we all went down for lunch after rehearsal. We're in the elevator and a woman comes in. "Oh, hi! Oh, it's so cold out! You know, it's so nice here. How are ya, oh?" Everybody just listened and when we walked out, Bill said, "I'm in." He got it so brilliantly.'

Macy wasn't the only actor with concerns of going over the top with their performances, of turning their characters into caricatures. 'Frances was very conscious of the dangers of excess,' Joel Coen would reveal, 'with that mannerism of dragging out words at the very end of each sentence.'

Aside from Himmelstein's coaching, the Coens also issued each actor with a handbook of sorts: the tongue-in-cheek *How to Talk Minnesotan* by Howard Mohr, a former writer and performer on *A Prairie Home Companion*.

In the book, Mohr disagrees about the sing-song aspect of the local tongue. 'Minnesotan is not a musical language,' he writes. 'Some people with an axe to grind have said it is the musical equivalent of a one-string guitar. What I say is, what's wrong with a monotone? At least you don't startle anybody. But it does mean that Minnesotans are not asked to be on talk shows as much as residents of other states. Not that we care.'

He also addresses the generous and plentiful use of 'you bet', describing it as 'a blanket reply on neutral ground'. Again, it feeds into that noncommittal part of Minnesota Nice. '*You bet* is mainly used to answer questions. If you can't think of anything else to say, "You bet". *You bet* is meant to be pleasantly agreeable and doesn't obligate you to a strong position. In fact, hardly anything obligates you to a strong opinion in Minnesota.'

Mohr also talks of the power of the negative in Minnesotan speech, of how it's used to avoid directly criticising someone. Marge's questioning of her deputy's DLR mishap – 'I'm not sure I agree with you a hunnert percent on your policework there, Lou' – is the most perfect example of this. Marge could have simply corrected him with 'No, you're wrong' (or much stronger), but instead points out the error of his ways with politeness and discretion. This is the way that Minnesotan speech hedges its bets. It talks in general terms, and with a confrontation-swerving, non-aggressive tone.

Hooker #1 talks in these general terms. To her, Showalter was funny-lookin', but she stops short of describing exactly what she thinks makes him so. It might be the teeth that his lips have difficulty containing. Or it might be the bug eyes set into those droopy, dog-tired eyelids.

But she tenders no actual opinion about his looks. Instead, Marge comes away with just that one nugget of information: that his foreskin remains intact.

TWENTY-TWO

'BLOOD HAS BEEN SHED'

Back in Minneapolis, Jerry is struggling to keep his mind on the job while he waits for an update from the kidnappers. He's in the middle of his rehearsed spiel with a potential customer, with those upsells – the sealant, the GMAC's finance package – fitted as standard. Then comes the call. The customer is abandoned, the sale potentially lost.

Jerry needs good news. He needs the abduction and the ransom payment to be the smooth process he's mapped out in his head. Answering the phone to Showalter, his cheery demeanour tries to will this to be the case. It's Jerry the salesman who takes the call.

'How's that Ciera workin' out for ya?'

But Showalter isn't up for idle chat about fuel economy or anti-lock brakes. He cuts to the chase. Blood has been shed, and he and Grimsrud are now demanding the full eighty thousand as compensation for risks incurred.

'Now we had a deal here!' Jerry protests. 'A deal's a deal!'

The tables have turned. He's now in the position of Bucky, that customer irate at him for switching the terms of agreement about the TruCoat sealant. And Showalter is now the metaphorical car salesman, the one squeezing more out of the done deal. Try as he might, Jerry can't claim any moral high ground here, not after making a career out of stitching up customers.

Not only will he be down that forty thousand (although, as we know, he's still siphoning off the lion's share of the seven-figure ransom, so he needn't be quite so aggrieved), but Jerry's now potentially implicated in three murders. The pressure is tightening.

The moment that Showalter hangs up, the phone goes again. It's a double whammy. Reilly Diefenbach at GMAC is back on Jerry's case, still chasing that paperwork for the loan. Now he's threatening for it to become a legal matter; his patience is at an end.

So is Jerry's. He picks up the desk blotter and slams it back down. Twice. Then – mirroring his glance up at Wade's office after his breakdown in the parking lot – he nervously looks out across the showroom to check that no one's noticed.

Appearances need to be maintained. After all, murder and respectability don't mix.

TWENTY-THREE

'HOW'S THE FRICASSEE?'

Minnesotan cuisine isn't known for its delicate flavours, for its light touches, for its mirepoix or velouté or beurre blanc. No one ever graduated from working the hot plate in a Swedish restaurant in Minneapolis to calling the shots in the kitchen of a Michelin-starred Parisian brasserie.

Food is fuel in these sub-zero climes. It's there to stop your internal organs from freezing up, at least until you can make your next visit, plate in hand, to the all-day buffet. Protein and carbohydrates are what's needed to get you through the depths of winter until spring's great thaw. Reassuring, homely, comforting.

The state does have some signature dishes. There's the Juicy Lucy, a heart-stopping burger consisting of two meat patties crimped together and filled with cheese, which, when teeth are sunk into it, weeps a lava of assorted fats. Then there's Hotdish, a starch-heavy casserole of potatoes, vegetables, perhaps some chicken and a sauce of cream of mushroom soup. For pudding, rip open a Nut Goodie, a candy bar of chocolate, peanuts, sugar and corn syrup which resembles what you might find in a cat's litter tray, but which is actually surprisingly good. I used to love them.

We never see Marge Gunderson gorge on a Nut Goodie, but she's clearly a fan of her home state's fare. Bearing in mind she arrives a third of the way into *Fargo*, she manages to pack a serious amount of eating into her time on screen. Marge only appears in thirteen scenes and yet we see her refuelling in nearly a third of these. That's a seriously impressive food-to-scene ratio. Sure, it's not *Super Size Me* territory, but filling his face and stomach was all Morgan Spurlock had to do in that documentary of his. He didn't have to squeeze in tracking down a pair of vicious killers between meals.

Norm Gunderson's food-to-scene ratio is also impressive. In his five scenes, he's busy chewing away in all but the last one. (To be fair to the big man, though, he's not actually eating in one of the others: he's already fallen asleep in bed with his hand inside a family-size packet of potato chips.)

It's clear that there's eating, and then there's eating the Gunderson way. Marge has an excuse for loading up the carbs, of course. There's a baby growing under that there uniform. She's got to nurse it through the winter until it arrives, bouncing and well-nourished, in springtime. Norm, though, has no excuse. Perhaps he feels he needs to be at one with Marge's condition – the culinary equivalent of a sympathetic pregnancy.

Marge is certainly no fussy eater, whether it's scoffing those eggs that Norm made her in the middle of the night prior to her inspecting the murder victims, or the Arby's take-out that he later drops by the police headquarters with. The only time Marge shows some discernment in her diet is when she's at the buffet the following day. (As the buffet consists of largely Scandinavian dishes, we can justifiably – in fact, we're probably legally obliged to – call it a smörgåsbord.)

Having piled the chicken and dumplings, the chicken fricassee and the Swedish meatballs onto her plate, she demurs at loading the torsk (as cod is known in various Scandinavian languages), neither the fried nor the broiled version. Let's not overdo it, eh? Her tray slides further along. As she scoops a big ladleful of an indeterminate pork dish, the camera pulls out, revealing TWO mountainous plates of food, together with a bowl of Minnesotan salad. It's the only salad that exclusively consists of bright-red Jell-O.

Norm's with Marge at the buffet, of course. For a man who takes a packet of potato chips to bed with him, there's no danger that he'd ever countenance missing a mealtime, even when his daily physical exertion extends little further than sitting on his arse and picking up his paintbrushes. At the buffet, he matches his wife ladle for ladle and the pair waddle off to their table: Marge because she's pregnant, Norm because he's trying to keep up food-wise. And he's doing very well at it too, his girth anything but that of a well-toned athlete.

Then comes a great pay-off. As the couple tuck in to their gargantuan helpings, they're interrupted by Officer Olson, here to deliver a potential breakthrough on the triple homicide. First, though, there's a catch-up with Norm.

'I thought you was goin' ice fishin' up at Mille Lacs?'

'Yah,' says Norm. 'After lunch.'

Boom. There it is. This huge meal – these thousands of calories, this coronary-in-waiting – is just to see the Gundersons through from breakfast to dinner.

Before Olson shows up, the couple eat in silence. But it's a silence that's far from awkward. There's nothing to say and no need to say it. As Ethan Coen notes, their relationship is 'based on the unsaid'. This meal remains a moment of intimacy, the pair sharing one of their true pleasures. They like their food. They're tucking in. Ever the gourmand, Norm takes a forkful of that Jell-O salad between chomps on a chicken drumstick.

Very few non-Gunderson scenes include characters eating. When they do, it's to further emphasise that theme of dysfunction, whether it's the Lundegaards anxiously picking at their dinner in the company of Wade the overbearing patriarch, or Grimsrud alone in the cabin, working his way through a TV dinner he's not really interested in, mouth agape at the news of an unexpected pregnancy on the soap opera he's watching.

For the Gundersons, though, food represents love and comfort. It's a medium through which we can see their inherent kindness, both for each other and for those around them. When Olson interrupts their buffet lunch and enquires about the quality of the fricassee, Marge is quick to offer him a taste. (That said, she doesn't ask him a second time, ploughing back into the piles of food in front of her. Even the new lead in the case that Olson has delivered is put to one side until her plates are clean. It's a case of priorities.)

It's a recurrent theme. There's great sweetness when Norm tenderly wipes some Arby's sauce off Marge's cheek, or when, despite his sleep-befuddled state, he insists on cooking up those nocturnal scrambled eggs. These are displays of simple, genuine affection rarely seen in the movies. We're programmed to believe that undying love can only be articulated on the big screen through grand gestures, usually involving one of the characters expressing their commitment to the other while standing in a rain shower of biblical proportions or at the departures gate of an airport terminal.

In those pre-dawn hours, we wouldn't have wanted Norm to show his love for Marge in such a dramatic way. I doubt Marge would, either. He headed for the kitchen instead. He knows the way to her heart.

And we need to take care of Marge Gunderson's heart. It's the pulse of the entire film.

TWENTY-FOUR

'I'M A POLICE OFFICER FROM UP BRAINERD INVESTIGATING SOME MALFEASANCE . . .'

As detectives go, Marge Gunderson is more Philip Marlowe than Sherlock Holmes, more Miss Marple than Mary Beth Lacey.

She is a lone ranger. She works best solo, no sidekick needed. Not for Marge the colleague off whom to bounce theories and motives, or with whom to dovetail complementary interrogation techniques. Her prowler's passenger seat remains empty. She rides alone, chewing over cases as she drives Brainerd's lost highways.

Marge is a logician, one whose deductions are informed by gut and guile. Whether or not it's because she doesn't have sufficient faith in her journeyman deputies back at Brainerd PD, she knows that the unlocking of this entire case – calculating the chronology, understanding the tangle of motives – needs a single mind. Marge trusts her instinct. It fuelled her rise through the ranks to the top job, after all.

AND IT'S A BEAUTIFUL DAY

And instinct is an individual thing. It's not the product of a committee. It isn't decided by a democratic vote among colleagues. It's singular, ephemeral.

Marge doesn't have the cool quips or acid tongue of Marlowe. Nor does she possess the intellectual narcissism of Hercule Poirot. But what she does share with them in spades is doggedness. She'll get to the bottom of things. She won't let go. Serious crimes might be short on the ground on her patch but, when they do occur, Marge gives them her full and absolute attention. And a triple homicide could be the case of a lifetime.

True to form, Marge rides down to the Twin Cities alone. Now, having checked into her hotel, she's arrived at her first port of call: Gustafson Motors. We didn't get much of an insight into her interviewing strategy when she was cross-examining the hookers; she was too mesmerised by the ping-pong of their conversation. But now, in an office overlooking the body shop, her sharp, to-the-point technique comes to the fore.

Although alone and heavily pregnant, Marge is far from intimidated or vulnerable when questioning the burly ex-con Shep Proudfoot. She's done her homework. She knows where he lives, she has the phone records for the property, and she's studied his rap sheet, giving her leverage when it comes to getting meaningful answers.

Armed with this information, Marge's approach isn't especially sophisticated. There are no intricate mind games, no point-scoring showboating. Her questions are straightforward. She seeks the simplest, most direct path to the truth.

Nonetheless, these questions do push Proudfoot into a corner, each one narrowing his room to manoeuvre. No stranger to a police department's interview suite, Proudfoot monosyllabically answers in the negative to each question, but Marge knows full well he took that 3 a.m. call from the kidnappers. He knows that she knows. She knows that he knows that she knows. With her cheerily disarming demeanour, Marge casually reminds him of how breaching his parole could put him back in Stillwater, the correctional facility out near the state line with Wisconsin. The wind has clearly been put up him. Shortly after the interview, Proudfoot disappears early from work.

If Proudfoot has plenty of experience of being interviewed by a senior police officer, Jerry is the rabbit caught in headlights when Marge suddenly appears in his office. That he's already nervous about her presence in the building is apparent before she steps through the door; he's doodling circles on his I ♥ Golf notepad with all the manic energy that his wife displays when chopping vegetables.

Marge introduces herself. 'I'm a police officer from up Brainerd investigating some malfeasance and I was just wondering if you'd had any new vehicles stolen off the lot in the past couple of weeks . . .'

Jerry's eyes tighten and he rocks nervously in his swivel chair.

'. . . specifically a tan-coloured Ciera.'

Silence – except for the squeak of the chair as it moves back and forth. He sidesteps the question, buying some time to think while asking Marge about Brainerd.

To us, knowing the depths to which he's plunged, Jerry's fidgeting displays all the signs of someone shifty and evasive. Marge doesn't see this yet; she has absolutely no reason to link him to the triple murders. She even makes a parting gag about his doodling when she leaves – 'I'll let you get back to your paperwork, then.' Right now, Proudfoot remains her target. She believes he's the one to lead her to the killers.

But things move fast. Marge will be back in Jerry's office soon – within twenty-four hours, in fact, and then she'll recognise the body language of a guilty man.

TWENTY-FIVE

'THIS IS MIKE YANAGITA!'

Marge hasn't travelled all the way to the Twin Cities just to check in on Shep Proudfoot and to make some enquiries of Gustafson Motors' executive sales manager.

A couple of nights previously, she received another night-time phone call while at home asleep. Thankfully, the caller wasn't a colleague reporting another triple homicide. Instead, it was an old high-school friend who, now living in the Twin Cities and having seen Marge on the TV news in connection with the murders, decided to call her up. They haven't seen each other for the entirety of their adult lives.

And he's rather exuberant for this time of night. 'This is Mike Yanagita! Ya know – Mike Yanagita. Remember me?'

Marge is dazed and a little confused. 'Mike Yanagita!'

'Yah!'

Marge is the embodiment of Minnesota Nice here. She's been awoken in the night, but denies she was asleep in order for Mike not to feel bad. Stilted conversation ensues, apparently to no discernible end.

But two nights later, Marge is entering the restaurant of the Radisson Hotel in downtown Minneapolis. She's interviewed both Shep and Jerry, and is now off duty. She's wearing the only dress we ever see her in and is touching her hair as she makes her way towards a man sitting alone at a table. She's clearly shy, showing all the signs of first-date nerves.

Agreeing to meet up with Mike is a combination of politeness and curiosity. And it gave her further reason to visit the Twin Cities. The combination of two Minneapolis-related leads – the information from the hookers about the kidnappers' next destination; the call to Proudfoot's apartment – and the chance to meet up with an old school friend offers enough reason to get out of Brainerd for the night.

But a calamitous encounter follows. After he makes an awkward pass at Marge, Mike explains how his wife – Linda Cooksey, another fellow alumnus – has died of leukaemia ('She fought real hard, Marge,') before breaking down into uncontrollable sobs. Feeling embarrassed, Marge suggests they meet up another time, but this just provokes more extreme behaviour. 'I always liked you so much!' he cries out. 'You were such a super lady!'

If tonight were any kind of romantic interlude (as far as we know, Marge hasn't told Norm about her dinner date), if it were going to lead into an adulterous subplot, Mike has killed it stone dead. We don't hear from him again.

Unsurprisingly, this is the single scene that has perplexed some of *Fargo*'s audience over the last quarter of a century. It's been the subject of deep dissection by Coenheads and Fargologists. And it's the scene most likely to leave first-time viewers scratching their heads afterwards, wondering – in such a tight, economical narrative – what on earth it was doing there. The more cynical members of the audience might even believe it to be filler to get the film over the crucial ninety-minute mark, like a novelist inserting an inconsequential chapter to reach their contracted word count and thus trigger the next payment of their advance.

Initially, the Yanagita scene has no obvious relevance to the plot, and Mike has no connection to any other characters. It's a diversion off the narrative highway, seemingly into a dead end. Why didn't the Coens just stay on the main carriageway? Reverse! Reverse!

But wait: the scene does have definite qualities. First, it's a highly entertaining aside in itself, with Steve Park's portrayal of Mike being an extraordinarily energetic and nuanced turn. As Adam Mars-Jones commented in the *Independent*, Mike successfully expresses 'a turmoil of feelings – grief, loneliness, desire – in a bewilderingly short space of time'.

The scene is also another display of Minnesota Nice in action. Marge is courteous, friendly and accommodating, until Mike moves to sit next to her, an arm sliding around behind her. The veneer is removed. Marge's annoyance is written all over her face, but she won't tell him he's out of order (instead, she concocts the explanation that his new seating position will give her neckache). Then, after a period of embarrassment on both their parts, it's back to the skin-deep pleasantries. Conflict avoided, move along now.

That said, the scene does represent a significant development in Marge's character, as Frances McDormand confirmed when, shortly after the film's release, she was interviewed by Willem Dafoe for *BOMB* magazine. For a short time, we see Marge beyond the context of wife/ police chief.

'I wanted to show how uncomfortable Marge was when he broke down. She is a cop, she can handle a lot of stuff, but when it comes to public displays of emotion, she was very uncomfortable. She had to leave. And, also, that just because she's pregnant, she's not this mother image. That was the last thing I wanted. If she was too sweet and understanding with Mike Yanagita, then it was gonna become too easy. And I wasn't interested in playing a "mother nature" type either.'

But it's the nature of Mike's character – one that echoes the film's major themes – that gives this scene its lasting significance. The next morning, Marge will learn from another old school friend that what Mike told her about Linda was a steaming pack of lies. It's then that she learns about the duplicitousness and desperation that can lie beneath an upbeat exterior.

As Jonathan Rosenbaum wrote in the *Chicago Reader*, the 'disturbing interlude' that this short subplot provides might seem 'awkwardly extraneous, but in terms of theme – a lonely individual lying compulsively, trying without success to hide his desperation – it registers as central'.

The following morning, shortly after discovering the truth about Mike Yanagita, Marge will begin to wonder if Jerry Lundegaard is cut from the same cloth.

TWENTY-SIX

'SMOKE A FUCKIN' PEACE PIPE!'

The precision of the Coen brothers' vision, and the tightness of both their plots and scripts, means there's little spare after shooting is completed. The cutting-room floor is never littered with extraneous footage that doesn't make the final cut. Negligible amounts of fat are trimmed.

There are only a handful of scenes in *Fargo* that, while present in the original screenplay, were jettisoned when it came to the final edit. The screenplay actually opens with Jerry arriving at a hotel in Fargo ahead of his rendezvous at the King of Clubs, checking in under the pseudonym of 'Anderson' (hence the police later calling out 'Mr Anderson?' when Jerry is finally captured at the motel in Bismarck, where he has used the false name a second time).

Also never seen was a phone conversation between Marge and Norm, when she was in the Twin Cities and he was off ice fishing. Aside from the fact that he wouldn't own a cell phone back in 1987 (and never mind the difficulty of getting a signal out there in the wilderness, in a little hut on a frozen lake), the Coens dropped this short set-piece as it didn't really advance the taut narrative. It was just another scene to reaffirm the closeness of the couple's relationship, a theme the audience would have had no doubts about already. Plus, the scene contained the obligatory discussion about Marge's latest meal – 'A place called the King's Table. Buffet style. It was pretty darned good' – but perhaps that was a helping too much. The viewer would have had a bellyful by then.

Then there was a scene with Marge and Detective Sibert, the Minneapolis detective who's been assisting her from a distance. Taking place in a cafeteria (of course!), the main purpose of this scene appears to be to draw together the dots of the case for both Marge and the audience. But the Coens don't like to join every dot. They enjoy leaving a little space around a plotline. And the narrative doesn't suffer a jot from this scene's exclusion – even if it does include the revelation that Mrs Gustafson, Jean's mother, is currently undergoing treatment for cancer in hospital. The assumption otherwise is that Wade is a widower. Had this scene been included, the fact that Jerry is at ease with putting Wade through the ordeal of having his daughter kidnapped while his – presumably terminally ill – wife is in hospital notches up his scumbaggery.

It might be controversial, but there is one scene that was included that feels extraneous, a rare breach of a plot otherwise notable for its bulletproof properties. And it's not one of the two scenes featuring that subplot involving Mike Yanagita.

After the awkward small talk between Showalter and the escort has dried up, and José Feliciano has finished his set, the pair get down to the real business of the night. However, this congress doesn't take place in a hotel room. Having been plying the escort with champagne at the Carlton Celebrity Room, Showalter brings her back to somewhere decidedly down at heel. The radiator's rusty, the walls are damp, the sheets are worn.

A third person soon makes it clear where they are. The arm of Shep Proudfoot wrenches the naked woman off the prostrate Showalter before delivering a fearsome slap across the kidnapper's face. How has Proudfoot found out that Showalter is in town, let alone where he's staying? Then it becomes clear. This is Proudfoot's home.

This makes no sense, for at least three reasons.

1. Proudfoot doesn't know Showalter. They've never met. As we know, Grimsrud is their mutual contact.

2. Even if they did know each other, why would Proudfoot allow Showalter to stay over, having already had Marge sniffing around? Showalter's presence, whether invited or otherwise, would directly link Proudfoot to the kidnappers.

3. Having hired an escort and plied her with Celebrity Club champagne, why would Showalter then take her back to Proudfoot's fleapit of an apartment rather than getting a mid-priced motel room for a few dollars more?

We've already been made aware that Proudfoot is a dangerous man (those 'entanglements' that Marge has found on his record), but the excessive violence he metes out in this scene feels unnecessary. Yes, it might be kind of satisfying to see that 'fucking little weasel' being given a good hiding, but it's superfluous and mystifying – as is the mauling Proudfoot also dishes out to his complaining neighbour out in the hallway.

The whole scene is illogical and without purpose. Had it fallen victim to the editor's scalpel, its absence wouldn't have created even the slightest hole in the smooth narrative. Its inclusion, however, does put a dent in the story.

The sole function that these sixty-eight seconds actually do perform is to turn Showalter, after a pleasant evening unwinding with a hooker, into a ball of red-hot fury. Being strangled with, and then whipped by, a leather belt can do that to a person. He's had enough and wants this whole deal completed. He makes for the nearest payphone and angrily calls the Lundegaard house.

'I want you with this money, Dayton-Radisson parking ramp, top level, thirty minutes, Jerry, and we'll wrap this up.'

The ransom drop-off is on.

TWENTY-SEVEN

'NO JEAN, NO MONEY!'

Jerry is back to being impotent, ineffective, powerless Jerry.

Since that meeting in Embers when, with Stan's support, he successfully forced Wade to stump up the entire million dollars, he's reverted to type. It turned out to be a one-off display of cojones. Having agreed to cough up the full whack, Wade had added a subsequent caveat: that he perform the drop-off himself. 'Dammit! I wanna be part a this thing!' he'd announced. 'It's my show here. That's that!'

Wade has grabbed the ringmaster's hat from Jerry; the man brilliantly described by the film critic Adam Nayman as 'the all-thumbs puppet-master' has been emasculated again. Of course, such an arrangement scuppers Jerry's plans even more than if the ransom had been cut to half a million dollars. He now won't get his hands on a single cent. And those two miscreants will get the full load, the entire seven-figure sum.

With Stan's floating vote this time siding with Wade, Jerry's plan has imploded. And when an irate Showalter calls the Lundegaard house to announce the location of the ransom drop-off, Wade is listening in on the phone in the kitchen. Before you can say 'Don't try to go toe-to-toe with a gun-toting madman kidnapper', he and the briefcase of cash are out the door. Key in the ignition, reversing off the driveway, speeding out into the cold, dark night.

Back in the hallway, Jerry raises his hands to the air and pirouettes in helplessness. He simply can't get his hands on that money now. The opportunity to remove nine hundred and sixty thousand dollars from the briefcase before handing over just forty thousand to Showalter has gone. But he'll follow Wade downtown regardless. He puts on his boots and tells Scotty he's going to Embers.

It may well be dawning on him that it's not just that the money has slipped through his fingers. There could be further consequences. At the parking ramp, Showalter might greet Wade with 'Have you got the money?'. Or, more dangerously, he might greet him with 'Have you got the eighty thousand?', alerting Wade to the fact that his own son-in-law has attempted to screw him over big style.

Or, of course, the handover could be uneventful, with Showalter only later finding out how much loot is in the briefcase. Then, there might be the very real chance of he and Grimsrud paying a return visit to the suburbs at an indeterminate point in the future, keen to show Jerry the level of their disapproval about the way he was double-crossing them. This disapproval would surely come bloodstained.

On his way downtown, Wade summons his inner Clint Eastwood. In an echo of Jerry rehearsing how to break the news of Jean's abduction, he talks himself through addressing the kidnapper. 'Okay . . . here's your damn money, now where's my daughter? . . . You, you goddamn punk . . .' Out comes a revolver, an indication that blood may soon be spilt. But whose?

At the parking ramp, the Ciera is parked up, waiting. Waiting for Jerry. Instead, it's Wade who pulls up and marches across with briefcase in hand, a sight that further enrages an already enraged Showalter.

'Who the fuck are you? WHO THE FUCK ARE YOU?!'

What was supposed to be a simple, pre-planned and peaceful handover of the cash (or, at least, of a much-reduced amount of cash) has now become an attempt at negotiation, at brinkmanship. At least it has on Wade's part. He wants to see his daughter before relinquishing the briefcase.

'No Jean, no money!'

'Drop that fucking money!'

'No Jean, no money!'

'Is this a fucking joke here?'

Since leaving the Carlton Celebrity Room, Showalter has had a bad night. He didn't get as far as he'd paid for with the escort, he's been strangled, beaten and kicked, and now some defiant old guy is attempting to play hardball. He's reached the point of no return. Out comes the pistol from his waistband and into Wade's midriff goes a single bullet. He falls back onto the snow-topped tarmac.

The bear gives his last growl.

It's Wade himself who ensures it's his last growl. That wound might not have been fatal, but when Showalter makes a grab for the briefcase, Wade pulls his revolver from his pocket and fires one off into his assailant's face. If he wasn't gravely injured before, he is now, as Showalter empties a few more retaliatory bullets into the old guy.

If we see *Fargo* as being a latter-day Western, this is the closest we get to a shoot-out between two gunslingers. There's no sign of the sheriff, though. But there might well have been. For the Dayton-Radisson parking ramp, as its name suggests, serves the downtown Radisson Hotel on 7th Street in Minneapolis – a location, trivia fans, just a couple of blocks from 9th and Hennepin, the intersection made famous by the Tom Waits song of the same name. But I digress . . .

The downtown Radisson is where Marge met Mike that very evening. Had they actually sat down for a proper meal and made an evening of it (we're safe in the assumption that the excruciating reunion lasted no longer than it took Marge to speedily polish off her single Diet Coke), Brainerd's finest may well have heard the gunfire, abandoned creepy Mike, and been called into duty.

Marge has presumably long since departed by the time of the drop-off and shootings. And Jerry arrives at the parking ramp too late to affect anything. As his car makes its way up to the top level, it encounters the Ciera on its way down, driven in a manner that redefines the word 'erratic'. After Grimsrud got to test its straight-line acceleration on that fateful night, Showalter puts its cornering through its paces, as he screeches and spirals his way down through the parking ramp's levels. He clearly wasn't listening during his first day at Crime School: don't draw attention to yourself.

A collision is narrowly avoided, but Jerry knows worse things have happened up top. He flips the hood on his coat, as if it were some kind of security blanket, and it's at this point that he undergoes a strange transformation. After more than an hour on screen, all nervous tics and buttoned-up anxiety, a strange calmness seems to flow through him. The panic has gone. He's greeted by Wade's lifeless body in the snow. But there's no wild emotion, no despair, no alarm. Jerry simply brings his car to a halt and flicks the switch to open its trunk.

The magnitude of what has happened has clearly dawned on him, the trail of death that his selfish scheming has precipitated. This realisation is heightened still further at the ramp's exit where he spies another innocent victim – the parking attendant, upended and dead in his cubicle. Presumably, like his counterpart at the airport, he attempted to uphold the minimum payment rule. Showalter's handgun won the argument.

Jerry stays in this new zen state all the way home. When he gets back, Scotty shouts to him that Stan has called twice, but he disregards the information with a cheery 'Yah, okay', just as if a Gustafson Motors receptionist was passing on multiple phone messages from an annoyed GMAC auditor.

He could run. But for now he chooses to go to bed.

TWENTY-EIGHT

THE SIGNIFICANCE OF PARKING LOTS

One thing I noticed when I lived in Minneapolis – and which I've been reminded of every time I've returned since – is the high number of parking lots and parking ramps across the city. The downtown area seemed to have at least one multi-storey ramp on every block; further out, there were parking solutions where no parking needed to be solved.

For instance, there was a parking ramp right across the street from where I lived, and another just around the corner. My neighbourhood – three miles east of downtown, squeezed in between the University of Minnesota campus and the Mississippi – didn't seem to have an overwhelming and pressing need for such generous facilities. The ramp across the street was a five-storey affair with, at a guess, in excess of 300 available spaces. I rarely saw cars either enter or leave. Instead, it was occasionally utilised by exuberant college students who, armed with giant catapults that needed two people to operate them, would fire water bombs from its top level at our building. One night, they hit their intended target – the window of my pal Joe, two floors up from me. The water bomb's terminal velocity was sufficient to fire it through two panes of Minnesota winterproof double glazing and a fly screen. The scene looked as though Carl Showalter and his crowbar had paid a visit.

Of course, with such plentiful parking options across the city, we should probably tip our collective fur-lined hat in Jerry's direction for managing to persuade the naturally cautious Wade and Stan that there was a strong economic case in putting even more parking spaces on those forty-two acres in Wayzata.

The Coens may well have also noticed the excessive number of ramps and lots across their hometown when they decided to make them a recurring motif throughout *Fargo*. Aside from being the subject of Jerry's proposed business venture, several scenes take place in this familiar urban environment, most notably that Roger Deakins aerial shot of Jerry dejectedly trudging through an empty snowy parking lot, having just received the brush-off from his father-in-law.

Showalter, of course, makes that fleeting excursion to the parking facilities of Minneapolis-Saint Paul International Airport to steal the licence plates of a snowbound car in long-term parking, while also choosing the crucible of the ransom handover – and thus the crucible of Wade's death – to be that downtown parking ramp.

And when he made the third series of the *Fargo* TV series, showrunner Noah Hawley extended the theme, casting Ewan McGregor as Emit Stussy, the Parking Lot King of Minnesota.

It's a typically contrary Coen touch to give something as prosaic as a parking lot such a central, pivotal role. It was to be Jerry's escape, the (legitimate) plan by which he was to make his money. Instead, it's where Jean loses her father and Scotty loses his grandpa. By gunfire, of course. Not by water bomb.

TWENTY-NINE

THE LOST BOY

Scotty Lundegaard isn't a bad kid. Sure, he's a little unfocused when it comes to his schoolwork, and he's susceptible to blurting out the odd profanity, but there's nothing that marks him out as being any different to any other kid of the same age in his neighbourhood. As an only child, he's probably been indulged a little more than he would have been had this been a houseful of siblings, but he certainly doesn't give off the arrogant air of being a cossetted, multi-millionaire's grandson. He even asks politely to be excused from the dinner table. That's better than most.

In the opening few scenes, Scotty's very much part of the family unit, but his presence diminishes as the film progresses and the plot thickens. The more Jerry fixates on getting the whole dastardly plan back on the rails, the less space his son takes up in his head. Jerry hasn't considered the distress that Jean's disappearance would have on the young teen. And it's worse than that. When Stan enquires about the boy's welfare, we're taken aback by Jerry's negligence. It's as if he's completely forgotten about him. 'Yah, geez, Scotty . . .'

When he finally does pay a visit to his son's bedroom, he encounters a tearful Scotty sat on his bed, finding solace in holding a cuddly toy close to his face. If ever a son needed his father, it's surely now. But Jerry remains distant, loitering in the doorway and offering little beyond the same plastic smiles he serves to his customers. No hug, no arm round the shoulder. Not even a ruffle of his hair. (In fact, other than the quickest of handshakes with Stan – and the police who tackle him in the motel in his final scene – Jerry has physical contact with no one else in the entire film. He doesn't even embrace Jean when he arrives back from his Fargo trip.)

Remote and aloof at the threshold of Scotty's room, his mind fixated on plugging the holes in this leaking scheme of his, Jerry says, 'So if Lorraine calls, or Sylvia, you just say Mom's down in Florida, with Pearl and Marty.' Then a retreat, another plastic smile, and the door closing behind him. Scotty is left to sob some more, alone.

This is the last time we'll actually see the young lad. In the last two scenes in which he appears – when Jerry leaves to follow Wade to the parking ramp, and when he returns home afterwards, presumably with his father-in-law's body still in the trunk – he doesn't actually appear. To emphasise the extent to which he's been disregarded, his presence lessened, you only hear him. He's now a disembodied voice coming down the stairs. He's been cast aside by his father, who can't step outside his own selfish bubble, preoccupied by extricating himself from this messiest of tangles.

Every teenager's innocence evaporates to some extent and for Scotty this would have been no different – had life in the Lundegaard house been a little less eventful, that is. Within a year or so, that whimsical poster of the Lederhosen-wearing accordionist on the back of his bedroom door would probably have been replaced by one of Mötley Crüe, for instance, or hometown heroes The Replacements, or perhaps a contemporary film. *The Lost Boys*, maybe, or *Hellraiser*.

But Scotty's loss of innocence understandably arrives a little too early, a process accelerated by his mother's abduction and the complete disintegration of the family unit. He retreats to his room to make sense of the whole frightening situation all by himself. No one seems interested in his distress or his opinions; his reaction to his grandfather's subsequent disappearance goes unrecorded too.

While the film is embroidered with other more conspicuous themes – greed, ambition, deception – the Coens' fascination with the definition of fatherhood is apparent. And that's unsurprising at this particular time. Two months after the film wrapped, Joel and Frances travelled to Paraguay, returning with Pedro McDormand Coen, their six-month-old adopted son. This was around the same time that Ethan and his wife Tricia Cooke also became parents – to a baby boy called Buster. The notion of being an effective father would have been at the forefront of their minds, and manifests itself here as an extension of the film's overarching good–bad split.

Jerry is unequivocally not a good father. Nor is Wade. His own daughter is demonstrably nervous around him, as confirmed by that phone call of his to their home. She's focused and articulate when berating Scotty for his worsening school grades, but as soon as Wade calls, she's back to being that bag of nerves she was at dinner the night before.

However, we're in no doubt that Norm will make a good father. He'll make eggs for Gunderson Jr whenever he or she is hungry. He'll wrap the kid up warm and take them ice fishing. And he'll put a paintbrush in their hand at the earliest opportunity.

The Gunderson offspring will receive plenty of nurture and love, but Scotty Lundegaard has been abandoned. Although one of his parents is still alive (albeit heading for a lengthy spell behind bars), the only child effectively becomes an orphan, without even his grandfather now to rely upon. Scotty is one of the lost boys.

THIRTY

'I DON'T ARRANGE THAT KIND OF THING...'

Showalter's mouth is what keeps the trail fresh for Marge. As we've already ascertained, he can't keep quiet. A chatterbox, a blabbermouth. It's almost as if, with that dental arrangement, there's not enough room left in his mouth for words and he's got to let them out.

But there's another part of his anatomy that ensures he and Grimsrud don't disappear into the snowy mist undetected. Just as he can't keep his mouth shut, Showalter seems unable to keep his zip up. His libido appears never to be satisfied, those below-the-belt impulses swiftly returning.

The pair were only a couple of hours or so into the whole kidnapping operation when those urges made their first appearance. Grimsrud only fancied another teetering pile of pancakes from the next roadside diner they encountered, but his partner upped the stakes, adding alcohol and paid-for sex onto the bill of fare.

Married to these sexual urges is a lack of discretion. Showalter's share of the ransom should have been reward enough to carry out a professional job, to be focused and undistracted. Sex shouldn't be on the agenda. He simply needs to abstain for as long as the entire conspiracy takes to resolve. Other than the odd waitress or gas-station attendant, the gruesome twosome should have avoided contact with anyone on the way down to the Lundegaard home, and on their drive up to the cabin with Jean. It was a simple task. But both of them – Showalter with his mouth, Grimsrud with his gun – have added unnecessary complications.

In casual postcoital conversation with Hooker #1, Showalter had revealed that the pair were on their way to the Twin Cities, information which was swiftly passed on to Marge, who then knew in which direction to turn her prowler. Yes, it might have been Showalter's mouth that effectively gave her this lead, but without needing to attend to that ravenous libido, there would be no hooker to blabber to.

Later, when he made his return visit to Minneapolis, ready to take care of the financials, Showalter again chose a wholly inappropriate moment to succumb to his sexual impulses. Despite the singular purpose of his second drive to the Twin Cities – the ransom drop – he still fitted in the hiring, the wining and the dining of an escort. And, until Shep Proudfoot and his leather belt showed up, the post-dinner sexual congress. This had been, at most, a few days since that assignation at the Blue Ox. Again, no focus. Too easily distracted. Too easily tempted.

Now, as Officer Olson steers his vehicle down a slushy residential street, we discover that, between those assignations at the Blue Ox and the Carlton Celebrity Rooms, Showalter had attempted to engage the services of yet another prostitute while on a visit to a bar near the remote cabin hideout. However, he discovered that those kinds of recreational opportunities were somewhat limited in snowbound, ice-sealed rural Minnesota.

The bartender, Mr Mohra, is busy sweeping melting snow off his driveway. Officer Olson – who, incidentally, in a continuation of the earlier discussion about winter outerwear, should be praised for his faultless deployment of the snorkel hood of his standard-issue parka – has rolled up after Brainerd PD received a potential lead from Mrs Mohra ('She heard about the homicides down here and thought I should call it in, so I called it in'). Mr Mohra then proceeds to tell the officer how, the previous Tuesday, a customer at the bar explained how he was going crazy out there at the lake and asked him how he could get some 'woman action'.

'I don't arrange that kinda thing,' was Mr Mohra's tart response.

Now comes the lead that will later pique Marge's curiosity and ultimately lead her to the cabin. After some bristly back-and-forth between Mr Mohra and the customer, the latter started to get threatening, boasting that 'the last guy who thought he was a jerk is dead now'. Again, the Showalter mouth couldn't stay schtum. 'That guy's dead and I don't mean of old age.'

Way to go, Carl. Discretion to the fore. Stay in the shadows, man. In fact, just stay in the fucking cabin.

'What'd this guy look like anyways?' asks Officer Olson.

'Oh, he's a little guy, kinda funny lookin'.'

'Uh-huh – in what way?'

'Oh, just a general kinda way.'

The description might be as imprecise as they come, but it's also bang on, matching that of Hooker #1. It's the verbal equivalent of two witnesses separately coming up with similar photo-fits of the same miscreant. In time, it'll certainly be enough to encourage Marge to take a drive out to the lake.

Two leads from nowhere. Two leads that will decide the kidnappers' fate. Two leads that Marge wouldn't be in possession of if Showalter had just kept those pants zipped up.

THIRTY-ONE

BURIED TREASURE

'Jeshush Chrisht…'

Those two words aside, Carl Showalter is stunned into silence. Something significant must have occurred to render him dumb. It's the morning after the night before, the night he despatched both Wade and the parking attendant. He's pulled up on the side of a deserted rural road to change the makeshift bandages on his facial injury. You can feel the pain as he strips off a bloodied section of kitchen towel before applying a fresh one.

Here in this solitude, he's allowed himself to look inside the briefcase carrying the ransom money. Perhaps he never expected eighty thousand dollars to weigh as much as it does. Of course, it doesn't. This is how much a million dollars weigh. He fingers the bundles with his bloodied hands. Jeshush Shrisht indeed.

Obviously, he's not going to share this with Grimsrud.

And it would be too dangerous to return to the cabin with this stack of cash in the car. So he removes the eighty thousand that's part of the deal, sets it aside and heads outside with the remainder, lolloping across the snowy roadside with an ice scraper in his hand.

Next to a stretch of barbed-wire fence, Showalter uses the scraper to dig a shallow grave and places the briefcase into it, before dragging a layer of snow back over. The briefcase doesn't need to be buried too deeply; he'll be back soon, once he's given Grimsrud his share of the cash and parted ways with him.

He looks right. The fence disappears into the distance. He looks left. The fence disappears into the distance. There's not one distinguishing geographical feature in either direction. He plants the bright-red scraper in the snow. That will mark the spot.

Another faultless plan.

THIRTY-TWO

'SIR, YOU HAVE NO CALL TO GET SNIPPY WITH ME'

Marge doesn't knock. She's on a mission and takes Jerry Lundegaard by surprise. Today, there's more steel in her stride, more purpose to her pace.

She started the day packing up her things in the hotel room while on the phone to an old school friend. This pal, Valerie, is the one who fills her in about Mike Yanagita. It turns out that Mike's version of his personal world is somewhat at odds with the reality. He wasn't married to Linda Cooksey, but he did pester her for an extended period. And, despite his portrayal of her losing battle with leukaemia, Linda is very much alive and kicking.

The truth knocks Marge back somewhat. 'That's a surprise,' she says, with gross understatement. She checks out of the hotel and starts driving back north, but the Yanagita episode is playing on her mind. Throughout her police career, she'll have had plenty of suspected felons being economical with the truth. That's par for the course. It's an occupational hazard. But, with such a faithful fella at home, she won't have been privy to outright lies tarnishing her personal life.

This sets her thinking. Should she be taking these Minneapolis types at face value? Specifically, should she be taking Jerry at face value? If someone she personally knows can so easily lie to her face, then why not a total stranger, a total stranger such as the executive sales manager at Gustafson Motors?

The Coens don't portray this point of enlightenment as a lightbulb moment. Marge doesn't cry 'Eureka!' and punch the steering wheel. Instead, it's the subtlest of changes to her expression – a frown and a tightening of the eyes that's pretty much imperceptible to the viewer unless they're looking for it. But it indicates there's enough doubt at the edges of her thinking to decide to turn the prowler around and head for a certain car dealership. Fortified by a roadside breakfast (and it's a good choice: what looks to be a Hot Cake Breakfast Sandwich from Hardees – sausage and folded egg between two thick pancakes), her brain is sharp, and she's got some questions that need answering.

Roger Ebert applauded the insertion of the minor Yanagita sub-plot as the device by which Marge replays her first encounter with Jerry. 'Imagine the Lundegaard interview as one unbroken scene, and you can see how much less effective it would have been. The delay between the scenes also allows us to imagine Lundegaard marinating in his guilt and fear, setting up his extreme nervousness when she returns.'

Jerry is busy with some genuine paperwork this time, resupplying those vehicle serial numbers for GMAC (and, by making those sharp pencils blunt, he's ensuring that the numbers will be as illegible as they were the first time round). He's taken aback by Marge's arrival. He's too engrossed in his fraud to see her closing in on him across the showroom.

Panic is in his eyes. It's all over his face. He's stumbling for words; his voice is breaking too. If Marge suspected there was something awry about him, his behaviour confirms her suspicions. 'Defensive' doesn't get halfway close. You don't need to be a chief of police to spot this is a man with something to hide. This is not going to be an evenly matched game of chess.

Unable to play it straight, Jerry shows all the signs of a guilty man, immediately losing his cool at an innocuous enquiry about how a count is kept of the cars in stock. 'Ma'am, I answered your question!'

A flick is switched within Marge. Miss Congeniality becomes Miss Jean Brodie. 'Sir, you have no call to get snippy with me. I'm just doin' my job here.'

Jerry tries to backtrack, to smooth things over, but when Marge asks to speak to Mr Gustafson, he explodes. The net is tightening, and he knows it – although it's his reaction that's doing most of the tightening.

'Well, heck, if you wanna, if you wanna play games here!' he snorts, before grabbing his parka and storming out to do an impromptu lot count. It will be the last time he leaves his office.

At this point, Marge doesn't have anything concrete to connect Jerry to the homicides. She can't yet turn disobliging behaviour into a charge of obstructing justice. But when she spies him driving past the window, speeding off the forecourt with a screech – 'Oh, for Pete's sake . . . He's fleein' the interview! He's fleein' the interview!' – the chief realises that's he tied up in all this mess.

Hell, even dopey Deputy Lou knows that only the guilty abscond.

THIRTY-THREE

'HOW THE FUCK DO YOU SPLIT A FUCKIN' CAR, YOU DUMMY?'

Carl Showalter doesn't need to bury the money. Carl Showalter doesn't need to go back to the cabin. Carl Showalter has a car and a million dollars in cash. He can go any sweet place he wants.

But he doesn't. Instead of pointing the Ciera south, east or west of Minneapolis and driving off to another life (with some plastic surgery along the way, to fix that nasty facial wound), he heads north, electing to return to the hideaway in order to give Grimsrud his split. Actually, he's doubling his partner's money, giving the Swede four ten-thousand-dollar bundles of bloodstained bank notes when the original arrangement was that he got half that amount.

What could be seen as an honourable deed is more likely to be an act of self-preservation. Showalter returns, presumably, because – as he sinks endless piña coladas and mojitos in various exotic climes for the rest of his days –

he doesn't want to be constantly gazing over his shoulder, expecting an angry Swede to be glaring at him across the bar. Whenever he got a whiff of Marlboro smoke, Showalter's heart would skip a beat.

So, surrendering an extra twenty thousand dollars out of his million-dollar bounty makes for a wise insurance policy. It's a great deal to buy eternal peace of mind.

But, even though he doesn't know his partner's shafting him, even though he's coming out of the whole bloody affair with twice as much money as he was promised at the start, is Grimsrud grateful? Is he hell. Is he happy? Not a chance. And when Showalter signals his intention to take the car as compensation for the various, often very painful situations he's been placed in over the last thirty-six hours, Grimsrud gets even less grateful, even less happy.

'We split that.'

'How the fuck do you split a fuckin' car, ya dummy! Widda fuckin' chainsaw?'

For the first time in the film – and despite knowing the dangerous double-crossing game he's playing – the audience's sympathy is with Showalter. If either of these hoodlums deserves a payday, it's him. Grimsrud has done very little in the entire operation, other than watching soap operas in a catatonic state and executing the initial murders that sunk them deep into this whole mess. And, of course, he's also brought a premature end to life for innocent Jean, whose freshly killed body – still tied to the now-upended chair – lies on the cabin floor. But now he wants the car (or the money to cover his share of the car), despite him only driving it for that mile or so down the road to despatch the witnesses to the trooper's slaying.

Showalter has been doing the heavy lifting – literally, when it came to dragging the state trooper off the highway. He's been doing all the back and forth. He's been beaten, he's been shot in the face. And he deserves an unequal payday. Justifiably, he flips his lid.

(Even in the heat of this dispute, the Coens couldn't resist inserting a little light relief when Showalter moans at how he's had to listen to his partner's 'fucking bullshit all week'. He himself, of course, is the undisputed king of incessant bullshit. Added together, Grimsrud's grunted words don't fill a half-page of the screenplay.)

Knowing how volatile and ruthless Grimsrud can be, Showalter might have been advised to steal away quietly into the night. But just as his way with words (or otherwise) has attracted trouble at every turn, his gobbiness will be his ultimate undoing. As he heads for the door, he unwisely unleashes a volley of insults towards his now ex-partner – mainly along the lines of 'You fuckin' ash-hole' – while also pulling his coat to one side to reveal his hand gun tucked into the waistband of his corduroy trousers.

Denying Grimsrud what he believes to be his rightful reward is one thing, repeatedly calling him an asshole is another. Indirectly threatening him with violence is almost certainly the worst thing imaginable.

As he stomps off towards the Ciera, Showalter hears the screen door of the cabin open and the crunch of another pair of boots in the snow. He turns just in time to see Grimsrud, in his thermals and trapper hat, bring down an axe into his neck.

Goodnight, Carl.

THIRTY-FOUR

SHREDDING THE EVIDENCE

There is one aspect of the entire *Fargo* tale that didn't come from the depths of the twin Coen minds, that had its origins in reality. Its name was the Eager Beaver.

In January 1987, an airline pilot/part-time police officer from Connecticut was arrested and charged with the murder of his air stewardess wife. It was something of a landmark case, the state's first murder conviction where no body had been found. In carrying out what he presumably believed to be an invisible crime, the suspect, Richard Crafts, had unwittingly left a trail of evidence that led to a gruesome truth.

From credit card records, detectives discovered that, in the days following the disappearance of his Danish wife Helle the previous November, Crafts had purchased both a new freezer and a chainsaw, and had also rented a wood chipper. After his arrest, a local snowplough driver reported having previously seen, a couple of months earlier, a wood chipper being operated in the middle of the night on the shore of a local lake. The discovery of human remains there (bone fragments, a fingernail, a tooth crown that matched Helle's dental records) and the recovery of a chainsaw from the water led police to believe that Crafts had killed Helle, storing her body in the freezer long enough to be completely frozen, before chopping it up with the chainsaw and feeding the body parts through the chipper. At trial, the jury agreed. Richard Crafts was sentenced to fifty years. The case, which took on national notoriety, got logged in the filing system within the collective Coen brain.

Crafts clearly demonstrated a level of preparation when it came to the disposal of his wife's body. But Grimsrud's decision to feed his partner Showalter into the cabin's wood chipper was a spontaneous one. He had the presence of mind to literally shred the evidence. He could have just buried the two bodies in the snow and skedaddled, but no matter how cold it gets in the northern states, winter will always be a temporary condition. Soon would come the thaw, and soon would come the undeniable evidence of his crimes.

Just a few feet away from the spot where Showalter is finally silenced, the means of dispatching the bodies is handily placed. It's fast, it's efficient, and it's ready for action. And it would become the film's overriding iconic image. The wood chipper.

The imaginative disposal of a body has intrigued film-makers and TV writers for decades. The public made the acquaintance of the concept of 'sleeping with the fishes' through the first *Godfather* movie, the euphemism for a slain body being discreetly dumped in a nearby waterway. And it's proved an effective way to get rid of a corpse (in fiction at least), as long as sufficient ballast is attached – enough weight to defeat the natural laws of buoyancy and thus allow the more carnivorous members of the underwater kingdom to enjoy some unexpected snacking.

In 1990, Luc Besson's *La Femme Nikita* included the dissolving of bodies using highly corrosive acid, thanks to the appearance of Victor the Cleaner and his briefcase full of clinking bottles of the nasty stuff. It was most famously reprised in *Breaking Bad*, where it became former chemistry teacher Walter White's preferred method of making his enemies disappear off the face of the earth.

In *The Wire*, drug gangsters Snoop and Chris Partlow are the murderous double act who hide the bodies of their victims in long-abandoned houses in Baltimore's most neglected quarters. There they cover the corpses in calcium oxide – quicklime – before wrapping them in tarpaulin and boarding up the buildings. While not dissolving the bodies in the manner of fast-acting acid, quicklime serves to halt the putrefaction process, so no odour is emitted, and thus the city's law-enforcement officers remain oblivious to this most gruesome of cemeteries.

Although not the product of the Coens' imagination, the wood chipper is among the most innovative ways that bodies have been disposed of on screen. It fits *Fargo* perfectly: a humdrum, everyday piece of machinery reclaimed as a tool of unremitting savagery.

'Joel and Ethan wanted the machine to feel both utilitarian and familiar,' confirmed Rick Heinrichs, the film's production designer, to *Entertainment Weekly*. 'We researched various wood chippers based on what size would frame up well for Peter Stormare. We had to hide the brand name because, after all, what company would give permission to have their potentially dangerous yard implement put to apparent deadly use? There was a chipper brand called the Wood Chuck on the market, so I called ours the Eager Beaver, painted it caution yellow, and put logos and hazard stickers all over it.'

When you first realise that Grimsrud isn't grinding down

a handful of branches but is in fact turning human limbs to mush, it is properly shocking. On subsequent viewings, however, when the viewer isn't so unsettled by the sight of the chipper spewing finely diced guts over the virgin-pure snow, a sense of delight can be had from the scene – especially when you know that it's Showalter's leg that's jammed up the machine. If it were the remains of innocent Jean, that sense of shock would never leave.

But because it's Showalter, there's a sense of retribution at work. Any notion of tragedy has been removed now we know who the leg belonged to. The loudmouth has been silenced. Silenced for ever. Total fucking silence.

Actually, soot-black comedy becomes the order of the day, with the sight of Grimsrud trying to force down the white-socked leg of his partner-in-crime with a log retaining an element of farce. As the *New Yorker*'s David Denby called it, the deployment of the wood chipper for these murderous means is 'an act so casually ghoulish that the only response to it is laughter'.

And it might well have been the perfect crime had Brainerd's finest not arrived on the scene before all the body parts had been turned to mush.

THIRTY-FIVE

'THERE'S THE CAR! THERE'S THE CAR!'

As Marge returns to Brainerd from the Twin Cities, she takes a detour to circumnavigate Moose Lake, checking out the lead offered up by Mr Mohra the bartender. Jerry's erratic, irrational behaviour from earlier that morning has thrust the whole affair wide open – even if Marge is still working out just how the pieces fit together. At this point, there's a disconnect between the bloodshed and Jerry absconding. She doesn't know the identities of the two perpetrators behind the homicides (the descriptions of them remain the sketchiest, after all) and how they link to him. If they even do.

With a statewide bulletin issued to find and arrest Jerry, it's the murderers who Marge has in her sights right now as she carefully steers her prowler along the icy lakeside track.

Cue our friend Lou over the radio. This time he's not adding light comic relief through unwittingly inaccurate detective work, but progressing the plot with an update from HQ, namely a call that morning from a concerned Stan Grossman. Just eight words from Lou allow things to start to slide into place for Marge: 'This guy says she was kidnapped last Wednesday.'

Of course, here in the comfy seats, we've all known of the conspiracy from that very first scene in the King of Clubs. Everything was laid out on a plate in that very first conversation. It was never a whodunit for us. Instead we watch the entire episode being unpicked by the professionals through a combination of instinct and happenstance.

This is 1987. Methods of detection weren't as sophisticated or as scientific back then as they are now. For instance, the first murderer to be found guilty on the basis of his DNA had yet to be arrested. Had the state trooper's murder happened in a future decade, then his body would have been the focus of close attention by white-suited forensics professionals. They would have found plenty of Showalter and Grimsrud's DNA on the body and – presuming, as seems inevitable, the pair both have lengthy criminal records – would have been able to match it with what's held on the national database.

Plus, the use of CCTV was nowhere near as widespread back then. If it had been, there would have been at least one or two fuzzy images of the pair from their arrival and/ or departure from various bars and parking lots. Even from the most unfocused of pictures, not too many people in the local area would be a match for this gruesome twosome.

Instead, Marge has only the vaguest of descriptions when hunting them down. But no matter how vague, it's what jemmies the case open. The imprecision of Mr Mohra's description contrarily chimes perfectly with the other 'funny-looking' observation already on record. This could well be Marge's man. And she shows the appropriate due diligence: every lead, no matter how unpromising, needs to be checked out. Nothing can be neglected. Hence the drive around Moose Lake.

This is unsophisticated, uncomplicated police work. It's simply joining the dots in the most direct way, based on both an experienced police officer's instinct and the public duty of concerned citizens reporting irregularities. Hunch and hearsay – these are Marge's best tools.

Mr Mohra might not have thought the episode in his bar worthy of getting a visit from the police (and praise be to Mrs Mohra for suggesting he call it in), but he's quite possibly placed the murderers in a specific location, at a point where Marge didn't otherwise have a clue about where they might be. Furthermore, his assumption that the loudmouth patron was currently going crazy out at Moose Lake, as opposed to White Bear Lake, leads Marge right to the cabin.

'There's the car! There's the car! . . . My car! My car! Tan Ciera!'

Lou is sending a couple of cars as back-up, but there's no way Marge is going to sit tight and wait it out, despite being alone and despite being in a less-than-athletic condition. She parks up and cautiously plods across packed snow towards the cabin, the whine of machinery filling the air. Gun drawn, she approaches the source of the noise – the wood chipper, which is spewing mashed-up bones, muscles, organs and blood across the snow, turning it scarlet. Unsure of what to make of it, Marge squishes her nose up at the sight, just as she might at a dish of indeterminate ingredients at a restaurant buffet.

Grimsrud is using a block of wood to push a human leg, complete with bloodstained white sock, down into the chipper's whirling blades. On hearing Marge's call of 'Stop! Police!', he hurls the block at her and makes a bolt for it, heading down onto the vast frozen lake. But Marge has his measure. She can't pursue him but, just as she's certain about her detective hunches, she's also confident about her shooting prowess. One shot to get her eye in, another to bring him down. The choreography has echoes of Grimsrud executing the witness who stumbled away from his upturned car into the snow, except that Marge doesn't aim for his spinal cord. She needs to take him alive. A bullet to the leg sends him face-first onto the ice. He's going nowhere now, other than the back of her prowler.

Of course, it might not have ended that way. The contrarian ways of the Coen brothers mean there's no guarantee that their heroes make it to the last reel. Marge could easily have become the eighth murder victim.

Let's look at the evidence, after all. She's on her own, heavily pregnant and pretty immobile, struggling to keep her footing on the slippery surface. She knows that there are at least two of them, so she'll almost certainly be outnumbered. And she knows they're armed and extremely dangerous.

'Stay in the car! Stay in the car!' yells the internal voice of the first-time viewer who has witnessed the dead-eyed ruthlessness that both suspects operate by. The wisest thing might have been to back up the prowler out of sight until the other squad cars arrived and sit tight. Hold off until the cabin was surrounded. Perhaps, in the meantime, shoot out the tyres on the Ciera (the sound of which would be drowned out by the wood chipper's whine) to seriously limit any chance of the suspects' escape from this remote spot.

But Lou knows this isn't Marge's way. She's not reckless, but she won't shirk a confrontation either. She's dogged and determined. He's sending back-up but elects to not even suggest to his boss that she waits until it arrives.

Fortunately, it all turns out fine. 'Why did you ever doubt me?' she might protest. Just as her investigative powers are way sharper than outward appearances might suggest, she's proved herself to be no slouch with a gun in her hand. Marge has made it to the final reel.

Not all superheroes wear capes. Some wear parkas, mittens and fur-lined boots.

THIRTY-SIX

'AND FOR WHAT? FOR A LITTLE BIT OF MONEY'

The capture of Grimsrud, in this vignette played out in the solitude of Moose Lake, has tied together several loose ends for Marge. She heads back towards town in her prowler, with an audience of one to hear her soft homily.

'So, that was Mrs Lundegaard on the floor in there?'

In the back seat, Grimsrud is his usual self. Mute, dead-eyed. Marge gives him time to answer, glancing into the rear-view mirror at his beaten face, behind the tight mesh separating them. Not that a response is expected.

'And I guess that was your accomplice in the wood chipper.' (Marge has to guess. She never has the pleasure of meeting the fragrant Showalter, let alone be able to recognise him from his amputated leg.)

Still silence. Marge has nailed the identification of the victims, but Grimsrud won't give her the satisfaction of acknowledging it. And we won't hear from him again.

We've already had his last contribution to the screenplay – the grunts as his body hit the frozen lake after bullet pierced hamstring.

This drive back to Brainerd ties off some loose ends for us, too. If we were in doubt about the moral of the whole bloody tale, Marge's monologue confirms it to be a repudiation of greed. Five deaths – at this point, Wade's fate remains unknown to the police, while the slaughter of the parking attendant back in Minneapolis will presumably be included in the final body count at a later point – all fuelled by avarice. Marge's rhetorical questioning continues, its purpose to clear and cleanse her thinking rather than elicit a confession from the taciturn captive. Every good cop needs to understand motivation along with cause, after all.

It's a soliloquy that not only folds together the crimes, but also questions the nature of humanity.

'And for what?' she surmises. 'For a little bit of money . . . There's more to life than a little money, you know . . . Don't you know that?'

Marge's monologue is calm and undramatic. She's taken the role of pastor, her sermon soothing us, the congregation sitting in the stalls. The *Guardian* film critic Derek Malcolm observed that 'one feels she could humanise a snake', while the *Boston Phoenix*'s Gary Susman was refreshed by Marge being 'the first movie cop in about forty-five years who's not neurotic, tortured, cynical, scarred or tainted by her brushes with evil'.

Her philosophy here might be a little homespun – innocent and naïve, even – but this is the scene of the entire film that reveals the true heart of the whole endeavour. A simple life can be the best life. Ambitions needn't be supersized. The world is enough.

A glance up at the sky. 'And here ya are, and it's a beautiful day . . .'

Her words now have a soundtrack, the duetting sirens of two police vehicles and an ambulance coming over the horizon, out of the mist. The shot of their approach mirrors that of the opening titles, when Jerry's car and trailer were hurtling towards Fargo. Carter Burwell's main theme returns too, rising up to a crashing orchestral wave.

These are the bookends of the film. We can breathe again.

THIRTY-SEVEN

THE BIG FELLA WITH THE AXE

Certain towns in the United States lay claim to be the home of something or someone notable – an invention, or a famous resident. This fact might adorn the 'Welcome to' sign on the outskirts of town, or an annual festival might be held in their honour. New Haven, Connecticut, was where vulcanised rubber was accidentally discovered. Lockport, New York, gave the world the fire hydrant. And, as any elementary schoolkid knows, Kitty Hawk, North Carolina, earns its place in the history books as the birthplace of manned flight.

Brainerd, Minnesota, is, as Marge confirms to Jerry in that first interview in his office, 'home a Paul Bunyan and Babe the Blue Ox'.

Paul Bunyan is a folk hero here in the northern states and over the border into Canada. He was the subject of a thousand stories, a fabled giant whose superhuman skills as a lumberjack matched the workload of a hundred men. His legend – and that of his faithful, curiously coloured ox – has been passed down orally across many generations, his reputation gathering weight as it inspired songs and literary works.

Appropriately tall tales abound about the man. That he dug Lake Michigan as a watering hole for Babe. That he singlehandedly cleared a two-hundred-foot log jam on the Wisconsin River. That the multitude of lakes across Minnesota – all 15,000-odd of them – were made by his footsteps.

Bunyan and his bovine companion have a recurring presence in the film – whether in conversational references or the multiple appearances of the giant statue built by the Coens' set designer – fuelled by the brothers' fascination with myth and legend. These are the themes, the foundations, upon which they balance their entire fictional tale.

A handful of miles outside downtown Brainerd lies Paul Bunyan Land, an entire amusement park based around the life of North America's most famous lumberjack. The centrepiece of the park, its crown jewel, is a seventy-year-old, twenty-six-feet-tall representation of Paul Bunyan. But this is more than a statue. This is an animatronic, talking – *talking!* – statue, one whose popularity appears not to have waned over the intervening years. (The fact that, as he speaks, he can recall the names of the kids paying him multiple visits on a single day suggests there's a man sitting inside, possibly with a piece of paper and a pen, employed in one of the most bizarre jobs in the whole state. 'So, what did you do today at work, hon?' 'Oh, you know. Pretended I was Paul Bunyan again . . .')

You would have thought that boasting an attraction loved by several generations would have cemented Brainerd's indelible connection with the giant lumberjack. But, while the invention of vulcanised rubber in New Haven is incontrovertible, calling a fictional character one of your own (and a fictional character, at that, with no discernible creator or author) is a different matter. The ownership details are imprecise. The lines are blurred. Accordingly, Brainerd is not the only Minnesotan town to stake a claim to the big fella with the axe.

A hundred or so miles north-by-north-west of Brainerd – at the other end of a bike route invariably named the Paul Bunyan State Trail – lies the town of Bemidji, which fans of

Noah Hawley's *Fargo* spin-off will recognise as the setting for the show's first series. Bemidji believes Big Paul to be theirs. Drive into town – on Paul Bunyan Drive, of course – and you can't miss its own tribute: statues of both Bunyan and Babe next to the lakeshore. Make that drive into town on particular days in summer and you'll see the local population wearing plaid shirts in tribute, or the more athletic citizens taking part in the Bemidji Blue Ox Marathon.

Other places try to muscle in too. Halfway between Brainerd and Bemidji is the tiny town of Akeley, home of the Paul Bunyan Historical Museum. In front of the single-storey building is another supersized statue, this time portraying our hero bending on one knee and offering an outstretched palm that's big enough for visitors to climb into, should they so wish, for a photo opportunity. And why wouldn't they? There's not a lot else to do in Akeley.

And it's not just small-town Minnesota that celebrates Bunyan. There are also statues of him in Maine, Connecticut, Oregon and California. I guess, with that impressive stride, the big fella got around a bit.

The Californian statue is the tallest of them all; at ninety-nine feet, it's twice as high as any other. But despite its dimensions, it doesn't exude even a fraction of the menace given off by the statue specially created for the film – especially at night when, suddenly caught in the headlights of the Ciera, it looks particularly demonic. It's a hell of a welcome to the town for the after-dark traveller.

It doesn't exactly ooze bonhomie during daylight hours either, looming out of the grey Minnesotan murk with dead-eyed foreboding. As Marge drives back into town, with her Swedish prey silent in the back seat, even Grimsrud appears chastened by its presence. He's been staring straight ahead the whole way back from the cabin but now, as the prowler passes the statue, he turns his head to take in the man with the axe. An hour or so ago, this was him, chopping up his partner's body with all the force that Bunyan reserved for the sturdiest red cedar or white spruce.

Finally, away from the distraction of his favourite TV soap opera, away from the incessant chatter of Showalter, the gravity of the situation and the depth of the crimes appear to be catching up with him. For once not consumed by a cloud of cigarette smoke, Grimsrud is beginning to see clearly now. His expression is still blank, but the first pangs of remorse might just be showing in his eyes. After all, with his mate turned to gloop, he'll be the one to exclusively feel the full force of the law. All that bloodshed is now on him and him alone.

Until he has a theme park dedicated to him, Grimsrud hasn't quite usurped Paul Bunyan as Minnesota's most famous axe-wielder. However, the film has superseded Bunyan when it comes to how a Brainerd citizen now introduces themselves to an out-of-towner. No longer is a fictional lumberjack and his faithful ox the reference point, as it was with Marge and Jerry. The giant has been felled. Instead, a fictional crime will provide the conversational filler. 'Brainerd, yah. Home of that vicious triple homicide.'

Or, of course, more likely it will be 'Brainerd, yah. Home of Chief Marge Gunderson.'

They should put up a statue.

THIRTY-EIGHT

THE SAFE HAVEN

The film could have ended there on the road between Moose Lake and Brainerd, with the cavalry arriving to salute and applaud their villain-capturing sheriff. But there are a couple of things to tidy up, so two more short scenes round off proceedings.

First, we need to catch up with Jerry, last seen wheel-spinning off the forecourt at Gustafson Motors. The police have caught up with him at a motel outside Bismarck, North Dakota, a near-seven-hour drive west of Minneapolis. That he headed in that direction suggests he may have stopped off in Fargo on the way. Perhaps he was hoping to reunite with Showalter and Grimsrud, and use his best car-salesman patter to recover some of the money. Who knows, he might even have gone looking for his wife. That would be a turn-up. But, perhaps after a couple of orbits of the town, and checking inside the King of Clubs, he headed out and off, further into the sunset. But the police will soon catch up with him. And a quick check of the trunk of his burgundy '98 may well offer up the missing Wade.

Jerry remains a schmuck to the last. When the officers bang on his motel room door asking for 'Mr Anderson', he's forgotten that he checked in under a false name. 'Who?'

It's one last confirmation that he's anything but a criminal mastermind. It was only ever going to be bad news for him. It was just that he could never see that. As the *New Yorker*'s David Denby observed, 'what interests the Coens is how foolishly people behave, and how little they understand of what they're doing'. Denby is spot-on; Ethan Coen confirms that Jerry is a person who 'can't project themselves a minute into the future or imagine the consequences'. He just couldn't tell the difference between a bad idea and an even worse one.

Then there's one last scene back in Brainerd. We've returned to the Gundersons' bedroom, the location where we first met them. It's a scene of contentment. Marge has solved the biggest case of her career and Norm has just learned that his painting of a mallard will adorn the next issue of postage stamps. 'It's just the three-cent,' he sighs.

'Hautman's blue-winged teal got the twenty-nine cent.' The couple are never smug, but they do know the value of what they have achieved and of the lives they lead.

'They're both doing what they're good at,' as Frances McDormand explained to TV host Charlie Rose. 'John Lynch, the actor who played Norm, and I had a little actor's story on the side: that they were probably both on the police force and she was better at it, so she moved up through the ranks because only one of them could in a small-town police department and he got to go home and do what he really wanted to pursue, which was his wildlife artistry . . . They're doing really well.'

This back story fits the relationship perfectly. Norm clearly knows the Brainerd officers well enough to be his former work colleagues, but not once does he interfere with the case Marge is working on. He knows she doesn't need his help. Instead, he indulges his passion for wildlife painting, counterbalancing this with happily undertaking the more domestic role within the household.

For a film with several unforgivingly brutal elements, this final scene could be regarded as mawkish. But it stays on the right side of schmaltzy because it's authentic and heartfelt.

Evil deeds may occur, but goodness shall prevail. As the film historian M. Keith Booker has observed, Marge and Norm's marriage occupies 'a genuine utopian enclave in which mutual love and understanding reign supreme, even as that enclave is surrounded by a world of violence and corruption. Indeed, it is the fallen world at large that makes the domestic space ruled by Marge and Norm all the more special.'

The breathing space that the couple's scenes provide – at home, in restaurants, in Marge's office – is utterly necessary to allow the viewer to temporarily escape the deceit and double-talk of the outside world. 'Marge and Norm gave the audience a safe haven,' explained McDormand in the documentary *Minnesota Nice*. 'And Joel and Ethan don't often give their audiences that in their movies – a safe place to hang out and relax.'

Marge and Norm's world is a place where material things don't matter a jot. It's all about – and the Coens make no excuses for the ultimate moral of the movie – love and comfort. How rich or how poor the Gundersons are is simply not an issue. It's all about the value of their humanity. Were it that the other characters could learn this lesson.

Jerry only ever has that one thing on his mind: money,

money, money. It's what has put him in that deep hole of his and it's the only thing that will pull him back out. Money is what obsesses Wade too, what defines him – whether making more or saving his own. And, of course, Grimsrud and Showalter suspend all notions of morality in order to get their bloodstained hands on the stuff, ideally enough to keep them in pancakes and prostitutes for the rest of their days.

Norm is the polar opposite. A man of modest means and modest ambition, he's the film's omega male. The difference couldn't be starker. A briefcase containing a million dollars has been the chief obsession for the other male characters. But Norm finds great pleasure in something of such little monetary value as a three-cent stamp. His is a far greater achievement than the trail of death the others have – either directly or indirectly – left in their wake. He is a creator. They are destroyers.

He's helped create life too.

He rubs Marge's belly. 'Two more months.'

'Two more months.'

The Gundersons have a bright future. Those arrested face bleak ones. Seven others have no future at all.

THIRTY-NINE

THE AFTERLIFE #1 – THE SURVIVING CHARACTERS

Its presence could have fortified the sense that the whole tragic caper was a true story, but there was no documentary-style update at the end of *Fargo*, nothing to inform the viewers what happened next in the lives of the survivors.

In its absence, it's left up to us to speculate on their respective outcomes. Here's a suggestion of what might just have happened between the events of 1987 and the film's release nine years later.

Gaear Grimsrud was tried and found guilty of five murders, having offered no defence in court by – of course! – pleading the Fifth. But he evaded the electric chair thanks to Minnesota having outlawed capital punishment back in 1911. The recipient of five life sentences, he currently resides at Oak Park Heights, the state's only maximum-security prison. He is the pen-pal of Nina Carlson, better known to viewers of *Fargo* as Hooker #2. The couple plan to marry.

Shep Proudfoot was charged and found guilty of conspiracy to kidnap, along with convictions for violence against his neighbour. He returned to his old stomping ground – the Minnesota Correctional Facility at Stillwater – where he works in the garage, maintaining the jail's various vehicles. He is due for parole next year.

After his capture outside Bismarck, **Jerry Lundegaard** was also charged with conspiracy to kidnap, along with multiple counts of conspiracy to defraud. In a trial that fascinated the nation, and at which his own son testified against him, he was found guilty on all counts and sentenced to twenty-five years' imprisonment, also to be served at Stillwater. His privileges as an inmate were withdrawn within a few months of being sentenced. Having landed a plum role in the prison kitchen, looking after the food store, he hatched a misguided plan to sell contraband potato chips to the prison population. His fellow inmate Shep Proudfoot was the one who notified the authorities about the illicit scam.

In the end, as Wade Gustafson once declared, **Scotty Lundegaard** did indeed never have to worry about matters financial. With his grandfather and mother deceased, and his father (who wouldn't have stood to have inherited a dime of his father-in-law's money anyway) under lock and key, the young teenager was the sole beneficiary of Wade's extensive will. The entire business interests of the Gustafson empire were now his personal property. Until he reached the age of eighteen (when he changed his surname to Gustafson), these interests were steered by the careful stewardship of **Stan Grossman**, the man who probably knew more about their intricacies than Wade himself. When Scotty reached adulthood in 1991, he announced the direction he wanted the company to move in: two years later, and still obsessed by ice hockey as much as he was as an adolescent, he built his own stadium and set up his own team, of which he is president and Grossman is CEO. Scotty's dream is for the Brainerd Blue Oxen to become an NHL franchise.

Norm Gunderson continues to paint the fauna of Minnesota. His work finally graced the twenty-nine-cent stamp in 1993: a particularly striking portrait of a red-breasted merganser. The couple's daughter, Norma, is now nine years old. Her interests include target shooting, ice fishing and Swedish cuisine.

Marge Gunderson remains the chief of the Brainerd Police Department. Numerous offers for her to apply for more prestigious jobs – in Duluth, in Saint Paul, in Minneapolis – continue to fall on deaf ears. She stayed put, despite relative peace again breaking out in her hometown. No more triple homicides or complicated kidnappings have since landed on her desk. After her handling of that affair back in 1987 (dubbed 'The Slaughters in the Snow' by the press), Marge travelled to Washington DC to be honoured by President Ronald Reagan, in one of the last acts of his term of office.

Wade Gustafson and his daughter **Jean Lundegaard** were buried next to each other, on a patch of land in Wayzata, recently acquired by Gustafson Industries.

FORTY

THE AFTERLIFE #2 – THE MONEY

When he stumbled back through the snow to the car parked on the hard shoulder, Showalter would never see that briefcase nor that money again. No one else connected with the conspiracy would, either. It had all been one long, futile exercise. No one got rich quick. No one paid off their debts. But several people lost their lives in the process.

In the film, we never find out what happens to the money. The assumption is that, once the snow melts away in the spring thaw, perhaps a local farmer will spy the black briefcase by the fence. On further investigation, the contents will be revealed to be a soggy pulp of what might once have been bank notes.

In 2001, fourteen years after *Fargo*'s supposed events and five years after the film was released, a twentysomething Japanese woman called Takako Konishi was found wandering around a truck stop in Bismarck, North Dakota.

Concerned for her welfare on account of her wearing a mini-skirt in the depths of a Midwest November, a truck driver dropped her off at the local police headquarters.

An officer there, Jesse Hellman, tried to find out what the woman was up to, but there were insurmountable language barriers. Takako's English was extremely limited and Hellman's Japanese was nonexistent. She pulled out a rudimentary hand-drawn map – a road, a tree – which she kept pointing at, all the while repeatedly saying what, to the officer's ears, sounded like 'Fargo'.

'I actually had never seen the movie,' Hellman explained in the 2003 Channel 4 documentary *This is a True Story*, 'but another officer that was in the station said that in the movie there was some money that was buried.' The pair figured that Takako believed she was holding a treasure map that would lead her to the booty that Showalter had buried.

The officers tried to explain, in the simplest English, that the film was a fiction, a fantasy, and that no money would be found in the snow. Takako was resolute in wanting to get to Fargo and so, with no crime committed and thus no reason to hold her at the police station, Hellman dropped her off at the local Greyhound station.

A couple of days later came news that Takako's body had been found in woodland near Detroit Lakes, over the border in Minnesota. Officer Hellman's card had been found in her wallet. The story grabbed the imagination of the world's media: a young woman, searching for imagined buried treasure, had been found dead in her pursuit of instant riches.

Only that wasn't actually the story.

It transpired that the last phone call Takako made, from her room at the Comfort Inn in Fargo, was to Singapore, to her former married lover, an American she had met back in Tokyo. Then a suicide note arrived at her parents' house that Takako had sent to them while she was in Bismarck. This, together with the discovery that she had made several visits to Minnesota in recent years, knitted together to suggest a tragic reality. Perhaps Takako had visited the area in the past with her lover and was simply trying to return to happy times in a happy place one last time. Perhaps her lover originally hailed from round those parts. Knowing they would never be reunited, she simply laid down in the snow and froze to death.

'An urban legend, that's what she became,' concluded Paul Berczeller, the director of *This is a True Story*. How strange, and how poignant. The loneliest of deaths transformed into something famous, into mass entertainment.

'The whole treasure story was nothing more than a Coen brothers-style series of tragic misunderstandings. Nothing more than the figment of an earnest policeman's imagination. Nothing more than a tale that people wanted to believe.'

But it didn't end there. In 2014, another film – *Kumiko, the Treasure Hunter* – handpicked elements of Takako's final days and reshaped them into something else. The plot features another twentysomething Japanese woman who, discovering a VHS copy of *Fargo*, regards it to be a treasure map in itself. She then travels from Japan to the snowy plains of the northern states and successfully tracks down the buried treasure. Again, Takako's lonely death had been exhumed for the purposes of other people's entertainment.

That same year, an alternative suggestion about the destiny of the briefcase full of cash was offered by the just-launched *Fargo* TV spin-off, in the fourth episode of its opening series. Throughout that first series, both show and film were connected by a series of references: haggling with a parking attendant, for instance, or the Fargo crime syndicate being based in a building called the Showalter Block. 'There were definite footsteps I was walking in,' admitted its showrunner, Noah Hawley, 'but they weren't the same exact footsteps that had been walked before.'

There were no shared characters or locations. Until that fourth episode, that is.

This episode – 'Eating the Blame' – chose to take the connections between the big and small screens somewhat deeper by entwining their respective plotlines. Although this first series is set in 2006, a flashback takes us to the events of 1987. A youngish husband and wife, with a sleeping child in the back seat, are driving across the frozen Minnesotan tundra. Echoing Jerry's delivery of the Ciera, their station wagon is pulling a trailer. Inside it are their entire worldly possessions. This is a couple clearly down on their luck, rolling the dice in search of a new life. The husband confirms they are running away from 'debts, screaming phone calls, bill collectors at the door'.

We soon find out that the financial straits in which they're plunged are pretty grim. The station wagon splutters to a halt. They've run out of gas in the middle of this wilderness; the husband had put his last five dollars in the tank.

He gets out to clear his head, to try to figure out their next move. A passing truck refuses to stop, speeding by and blowing him to the ground. With his face on the icy tarmac, a prayer is offered up for any kind of godly intervention. 'I'll be your humble servant for the rest of my days.'

From his prone position, the husband – Stavros Milos – spies a red ice scraper sticking out of the ground next to a barbed-wire fence. He approaches it. Is this some kind of sign? If so, what is God expecting him to do with it? He starts frantically pawing away at the snow with the scraper, with all the intensity of Jerry chopping away at the ice of his windshield. Stavros uncovers the briefcase and is as astounded as Showalter was at its contents. It's only been a few days since the money was buried; the bank notes are not yet a pulpy mess.

This scene is not, like the rest of the TV series' interweaving plot lines, an at-arm's-length tribute. It's an extension of the story. As such, it needed to dovetail exactly with the original, despite being filmed over the border in Canada. 'We shot it in Calgary,' explained Noah Hawley, 'but we went frame by frame. We had stills of each frame, the angles they shot from. We tried to re-create it as close to the movie as possible. We had to match the fence. We looked for an area without a fence and then we put in our own fence. We also had to match the ice scraper. We found the right one, but it had a different blade. I think the one that they used in the movie was clear, and we had a white one. So we had to have it made specifically.'

That money never rescued Jerry from his bottomless debts, but it did transform the life of Stavros Milos and his young family. Nine hundred and twenty thousand dollars can do that to someone. Settling in Duluth, Stavros subsequently became a groceries magnate, his empire landing him the title 'the Supermarket King of Minnesota'. The life-changing ice scraper is framed on his wall.

But, nearly twenty years after stumbling upon the cash, there's something rotten in the state of Stavros. He's the target of a blackmailing conspiracy, with the blackmailer sending him messages that suggest they know the source of that start-up money and demanding a million dollars to keep them quiet. Dangerous people might be on his tail – possibly the original owners of the buried briefcase out for revenge. Knowing that, since the miracle on the roadside two decades back, Stavros is a devoutly religious man, the blackmailer (Billy Bob Thornton's Lorne Malvo) sets up a series of acts of God to scare him into submission: the release of locusts in one of his stores is one, putting pigs' blood in his shower plumbing is another. These episodes convince Stavros to reverse his actions from all those years ago: he fills the briefcase with a million dollars from the company coffers and buries it again on that same patch of snowy roadside.

It's an action that, tantalisingly, keeps the conundrum alive. That cursed money may still be out there.

FORTY-ONE

THE AFTERLIFE #3 – THE ACTORS

Once the snow melted and the blood was washed away, Fargo's actors went their separate ways, getting on with the business of more auditions and more film sets.

So what happened next for the principal players?

Born in Brooklyn to Korean parents, **Steve Park** worked as a stand-up comedian before moving into acting. Prior to bringing highly-strung Mike Yanagita to life, Park's early work included being a cast member of the TV sketch show *In Living Color* and having roles in films such as Spike Lee's *Do the Right Thing* and the Michael Douglas-starring *Falling Down*. In 1997, he wrote what he called a 'mission statement', prompted to do so by witnessing derogatory remarks made towards another Asian actor on the set of *Friends*. Park described working on the show as 'an extremely painful experience', as he had encountered 'a disturbing lack of generosity of spirit and basic human courtesy'. Pleasingly, he also noted that 'working with the Coen brothers and Frances McDormand was one of the high points of my career – not so much because they are brilliant artists, but because they are decent, down-to-earth people who treated me and the rest of the cast and crew with respect and admiration'. Park returned to Minnesota, again in the company of the Coens, by playing the role of Clive's father in *A Serious Man*.

Since *Fargo*, **Bruce Bohne** – the man behind Lou, the dopey deputy – has split his time between stage and screen. He's had a number of small movie roles, among them appearances in the remake of *Dawn of the Dead*, *Jingle All the Way*, *Patch Adams* (where, incidentally, the cast also included Harve 'Wade Gustafson' Presnell) and the Minnesota-set *North Country*. Bohne's TV work has included roles in *Law & Order: Special Victims Unit* and *Star Trek: Voyager*.

A member of the Blackfoot tribe, **Steven Reevis** was cast in a number of Native American roles in movies before landing the part of Shep Proudfoot, among them *Dances with Wolves*, *Geronimo: An American Legend* and *Last of the*

Dogmen. The two days he spent on the Fargo set – one day shooting the scenes in the workshop at Gustafson Motors, the other 'where I end up getting violent with Steve Buscemi' – would be his most conspicuous acting roles, as he later acknowledged. 'That's the only film that people recognise me from when I'm walking down the street.' Despite his limited time on set, the Coens made an impression on Reevis. 'They really know their craft,' he noted. 'They're kind of different. Joel, he's more serious, and Ethan gets excited when he sees a scene and really likes it.' Reevis never got to work with the brothers again. He died in Montana in December 2017, leaving behind a wife, four children and three grandchildren.

Only fourteen years old at the time of playing Scotty Lundegaard, like many other of the cast's supporting actors *Fargo* remains Minneapolis native **Tony Denman**'s cinematic high point to date. 'I was too young at the time to really understand the incredible talent of the Coen brothers,' he later observed, 'and just how much this movie would mean to the history of cinema and the effect it would have on people.' Now in his forties, Denman continued his acting career into adulthood, appearing – among other roles – in several movies in the *National Lampoon* franchise. He looks back fondly on *Fargo*, glad that he trusted his adolescent instincts and not parental advice. 'My dad did tell me years later that, when he initially read the script, he thought it was awful.

Denman's on-screen mother, **Kristin Rudrüd**, was the one Fargo native in the cast; she still lives there today. On the back of playing mildly neurotic housewife Jean Lundegaard, several film roles came her way, including *Pleasantville* (which also starred William H. Macy) and *Drop Dead Gorgeous*. Like *Fargo*, both films were set in small Midwest towns, the latter in fictional Mount Rose, Minnesota. But, as Rudrüd explained on an episode of the radio show *A Prairie Home Companion*, she continues to be remembered for her sole Coen brothers film – even though there's often a case of mistaken identity when people approach her in person. 'That was pretty funny when you went through the wood chipper there . . .'

John Carroll Lynch is another of the supporting cast who's appeared in other Minnesota-set films. In his case, two others were released the same year as *Fargo*: he played a bartender in the Matt Dillon-starring *Beautiful Girls* and a cop in the

Keanu Reeves/Cameron Diaz vehicle *Feeling Minnesota*. But it was his turn as Norm 'Son of a' Gunderson that was the meatiest role of all three. '*Fargo* was the turnaround for me,' he later confirmed, 'because it was a part. It wasn't a line.' More proper roles followed, including being directed by Clint Eastwood in *Gran Torino* and Martin Scorsese in *Shutter Island*. Lynch has rarely been out of work in the last quarter-century. And he's also ventured to the other side of the camera, directing nonagenarian Harry Dean Stanton in one of his final roles in 2017's *Lucky* (a film in which he also had to direct a scene featuring his namesake David Lynch. No pressure there, then).

Although he's a native Minnesotan, unlike the other local actors cast by the Coens, **Larry Brandenburg** already had some experience of Hollywood by the time the *Fargo* cast and crew landed in his home state and he turned into Stan Grossman. He had minor appearances in two Kevin Costner movies under his belt – *The Untouchables* and *Field of Dreams* (in the former, he plays a reporter quizzing Robert De Niro's Al Capone over his use of violence; in the latter, he's a heckler at a school PTA meeting). He then landed the role of Skeet in *The Shawshank Redemption*, in which he worked with *Fargo* cinematographer Roger Deakins for the first time. Since *Fargo*, Brandenburg has mainly worked in television, including roles in *The West Wing*, *John from Cincinnati*, *Grey's Anatomy* and *Star Wars: The Clone Wars*. He has also played no fewer than three different characters in *NYPD Blue*.

For a dedicated man of the stage, Fargo marked **Harve Presnell**'s first film role for twenty-seven years, since *Paint Your Wagon* in 1969. But it was far from his last; following his tough-as-a-nut performance as Wade Gustafson, Presnell found himself in high demand with directors who needed a belligerent senior citizen with undeniable screen presence. His post-*Fargo* cinematic highlights included turns in *Face/Off*, *Saving Private Ryan* and *Evan Almighty*. The latter was his final role before he succumbed to pancreatic cancer in 2009 at the age of seventy-five.

'*Fargo* was the one that really opened a lot of doors for me,' **Peter Stormare** told *Empire* magazine of his time with the Coens. 'I've only worked with them the two times. They say we're going to do something else together, so hopefully.' Stormare was actually on course for making his first appearance for the brothers in *Miller's Crossing*, in a part specially written for him – a hitman known as The Swede, but his commitments to the National Theatre back in Sweden got in the way. Stormare followed up his portrayal of Gaear Grimsrud two years later in *The Big Lebowski*, in which he played Uli the nihilist. In a neat touch, as Uli he enjoyed a scene in a diner in which he successfully ordered some lingonberry pancakes – the foodstuff Steve Buscemi tried to prevent him having on the road to Minneapolis in favour of a steak and a beer and a shot. Stormare has chalked up a string of appearances in the biggest blockbusters – *The Lost World: Jurassic Park*, *Armageddon*, *Minority Report*, *Bad Boys II*, *John Wick: Chapter 2* – as well as a parallel career as a part-time musician. The name of his band? Blonde From Fargo.

Steve Buscemi appeared in five consecutive Coen brothers films, yet all but one of his characters failed to make it to the final credits. Being killed off is 'my kind of forte' he joked to talk-show host Stephen Colbert. 'Sometimes, when I read a script, I just go to the end to see how I die.' In addition to his disappearance into the wood chipper, as

Mink Larouie in *Miller's Crossing* he is fatally shot in the face; as Chet the bellboy in *Barton Fink*, he expires in the hotel fire; and as quiet, meek Donny in *The Big Lebowski*, he suffers a fatal heart attack with just a couple of scenes to go. Only in *The Hudsucker Proxy*, in a tiny role as a bartender in a beatnik bar, does he escape the grim reaper's blade. His death in *The Big Lebowski* has a neat connection with *Fargo*: Buscemi was again killed off by Stormare, albeit indirectly having suffered a cardiac arrest after the nihilists' laughable attack on The Dude and his pals in the parking lot outside the bowling alley. Described as 'the master misfit' by the *Telegraph*, Buscemi has rarely had a day off in a forty-year acting career, including playing the prestige roles of Tony Blundetto in *The Sopranos* and 'Nucky' Thompson in *Boardwalk Empire*. Arguably, though, former firefighter Buscemi's most significant post-*Fargo* role was when, the day after 9/11, he voluntarily returned to his old company, Engine Company 55, to work five ten-hour days searching through the rubble of the Twin Towers.

'I was born to play that role,' **William H. Macy** announced of his career-defining turn as Jerry Lundegaard. It earned him an Academy Award nomination in the Best Supporting Actor category alongside the likes of Edward Norton and James Woods, although they all lost out to *Jerry Maguire*'s Cuba Gooding Jr. If he is still best remembered as Lundegaard, Macy doesn't show an ounce of resentment towards being defined by a twenty-five-year-old role. His CV boasts subsequent appearances in some A-grade films – *Magnolia, Boogie Nights, The Cooler, Welcome to Collingwood* – along with the lead role in the US remake of UK comedy-drama *Shameless*. Pestering the Coens to cast him has given him a life less ordinary. '*Fargo* was a demarcation point in my career,' he admitted to *Entertainment Weekly*. 'I didn't need to audition after that. I owe them everything.'

The actor who has enjoyed the most decorated post-Fargo career is undoubtedly **Frances McDormand**. But, unlike Macy or Stormare, the film didn't mark a particular threshold over which she passed. McDormand's acting had already caught the eye of the Academy Award jury (with a nomination for Best Supporting Actress for 1988's *Mississippi Burning*) before she won the Best Actress Oscar for her performance of Marge Gunderson, holding off the likes of

Diane Keaton, Brenda Blethyn, Kristin Scott Thomas and
Emily Watson. Three further Academy Award nominations
would follow – for *Almost Famous*, *North Country* and *Three
Billboards Outside Ebbing, Missouri* – the final one bagging
her second Oscar, along with a Golden Globe and a BAFTA.
Not that she has ever courted celebrity. 'I've never been a
personality,' she explained to the *Guardian* when dissecting
the secret of her success. 'I've always been a character actor.
I think it's also about people not knowing who I am.' But
no matter McDormand's shape-shifting qualities, she was a
little disappointed when husband Joel and brother-in-law
Ethan handed her the bespoke role of Marge. 'When I read
the script, I was like "Okay, all right. Marge, a Midwestern
cop",' she later recalled. 'At the time, I thought psychopath,
a killer, a whore. Something with a little more meat to it. It
wasn't until I really got into the process that I realised how
much fun I was going to have.'

The fun extended far and wide. After the huge losses
sustained by its immediate predecessor *The Hudsucker Proxy*,
Fargo's box-office take was in excess of sixty million dollars,
delivering the kind of profit on its seven-million-dollar

budget that would have crotchety old Wade Gustafson purring with delight. Those numbers look pretty sweet . .

The film's critical acclaim was even heftier. Roger Ebert called it 'one of the best films I've ever seen', singling out the Coens for their daring and their genius. 'To watch it is to experience steadily mounting delight, as you realise the filmmakers have taken enormous risks, gotten away with them and made a movie that is completely original, and as familiar as an old shoe.'

Fargo was nominated for the Palme d'Or at Cannes, and the screenplay saw the brothers win their first Oscar. Weighed down by praise and adulation, the Coens never got carried away. 'It was never an ambition to grow up and win an Academy Award,' Ethan would joke, 'so when it happens, you go "Weird!".'

The haul – both in terms of silverware and in cash receipts – wasn't bad for a film that, without Jeff Bridges's diary being so crammed, might never have been written. *The Big Lebowski*, the brothers' intended project after *The Hudsucker Proxy*, had been put on ice while its main star cleared his schedule. So the Coens went off and wrote *Fargo* instead. Thanks, Jeff.

FORTY-TWO

RETURN TO FARGO

We end our journey where the film nominally began. And bearing in mind that fewer than five minutes of the whole affair are set outside Minnesota, North Dakota did pretty well out of *Fargo*.

The intention was that all the scenes would be shot on the Minnesotan side of the state line, including the two North Dakota-set scenes. Aside from the neighbourhood bar in north-east Minneapolis that doubled as the King of Clubs, the motel where Jerry is arrested is actually in Forest Lake, Minnesota, four hundred and fifty miles east of its supposed location 'outside Bismarck, North Dakota'.

In the end, thanks to the unusually mild weather of the winter of 1995 which forced the *Fargo* crew northwards in search of significant snowfall to film in, North Dakota did get its moment in front of the cameras. Many of the scenes requiring deep snow were filmed in the north-eastern corner of the state, including the crucial scene involving that 'execution-type deal'. (For several of the Minnesota-shot scenes, the crew were forced to truck in snow, such was the scarcity of the white stuff.)

And, of course, North Dakota gave the film its name, despite only that opening scene being set in the titular town. 'Fargo seemed a more evocative title than Brainerd,' explained Joel Coen. 'That's the only reason.' Ethan backed him up. 'It was just that we liked the sound of the word. There's no hidden meaning.'

And Brainerd also seems to have lost out when it comes to the film's legacy. The western half of the twin cities of Fargo-Moorhead (the latter being on the Minnesotan side of the Red River), Fargo has more warmly embraced the marketing opportunities offered by its connection to a much-loved film, despite all its violence and gore. But with all the bloodshed occurring across the state line – and with the accent that's mildly lampooned being the Minnesotan one, not the North Dakotan – I guess it makes for a more palatable prospect with which to snag the tourist dollar. Perhaps Brainerd deliberately kept its distance.

Curiously, the Fargo-Moorhead Visitors Center is located

out by I-94, some way from the downtown area. In its favour, it is housed in arguably the most impressive building in which a tourist information centre could be found – a magnificent, towering old grain silo. Pull off the interstate and into the parking lot, though, and an even more notable sight is visible through the window on the passenger side.

It is a piece of genuine cinema memorabilia. Mounted on a concrete circle, guarded by a ring of knee-high ferns, sits the yellow peril itself. The blood-hungry monster. The scourge of Showalter. Yes, it's the – *the!* – wood chipper.

Its location isn't the best in which to protect a cultural artefact of such renown. It's not only open to the worst weather that the North Dakota weather gods can chuck at it (and the vehicle fumes floating over from the interstate), but it also regularly has a gaggle of tourists clambering all over it, mugging up for the camera. Sure, the chipper's presence in the film is all to do with destruction and disposal, but this seems an unsightly way for the old girl to see out her days.

But relax. This is merely a replica. The original chipper, complete with its bespoke Eager Beaver decals and signed by the Coens, is inside the visitors' centre, out of the salty elements. Indoors, though, there's also a regular gaggle of tourists also grabbing their photo opportunities. And here the centre's staff assist them, lending them trapper hats to impersonate Grimsrud as they pretend to push a prosthetic leg into the vicious teeth of the machine.

For those avoiding such cheesy moments, the film does manifest itself in several ways here. Posters adorn the walls, and there's a signed, original – and decidedly weather-beaten – script to peruse. And then there are the retail opportunities, with wood chipper-branded gifts galore. T-shirts, sweatshirts, hats, mugs, shot glasses, coasters, fridge magnets . . . You can even buy a miniature yellow wood chipper ornament to hang from your Christmas tree. Festive? You betcha!

The visitors' centre isn't Fargo's only acknowledgement of the movie that bears its name. In 2006, on the tenth anniversary of its release, the film was projected onto the outside wall of the thirteen-storey Radisson Hotel, at that time the tallest building in Fargo. Third Avenue North was closed to traffic and turned into a giant parking lot, while residents on the north side of the hotel could watch from their windows. However, because the city tsars couldn't allow the frequent profanities to waft across the skyline, viewers had to tune into local radio station KPFX 107.9 to hear the audio track. It would be a celebration of the film. 'The night is going to be about the larger-than-life effect the movie has had on Fargo,' gushed the organiser ahead of the showing, the suitably named Margie Bailly, who founded the Fargo Film Festival and who, at the time, also ran the art deco Fargo Theater downtown. (The theatre, I'm pleased to report, boasts a life-sized wooden carving of Chief Gunderson.)

There is, though, a surprising reluctance in the business owners downtown to cash in on the film's success. For instance, if I were the proprietor of Deek's Pizza on North University Drive, I'd certainly be theming my offerings accordingly – the Showalter Supreme, the Grimsrud Gutbuster, the Lundegaard Lunch Deal.

Similarly, it's kind of disappointing that the hipster-friendly Proof Artisan Distillery on 4th Avenue North hasn't named its high-proof spirits along these lines either. Jerry's Gin and Wood Chipper Whiskey are crying out to be put on the shelves. Tricks are being missed here. Simple marketing, isn't it?

At the Boiler Room, the popular bar/restaurant down Roberts Alley, there is at least a possible acknowledgement of the film's existence on the menu. And certainly Marge's World Famous Hotdish – ground bison, rich gravy, green beans, carrots and corn, topped with cheese and three-cheese tator tots – would be welcomed any time on a certain police chief's plate.

FORTY-THREE

AND MORE BESIDES...

Jerry Lundegaard was almost certainly named after **Bob Lundegaard**, the long-serving local film critic whose reviews in Twin Cities newspaper the *Star Tribune* the Coens would have read voraciously in the 1970s (he panned the first *Star Wars* movie in 1977. 'Don't bring your brains with you' was the memorable advice he gave his readers). At *Fargo*'s premiere, Lundegaard asked the Coens if Jerry was named after him. The brothers, at that point still keen to blur the lines of the film's fact and fiction, denied he had been the inspiration: 'No, it's a common name.'

The eagle-eyed will have spotted that, in the closing credits, the actor playing '**Victim in Field**' (aka the driver who inadvertently sees Showalter hauling the state trooper's body off the highway) is represented by a squiggle rather than a name. At the time, this caused excitement among

Coenheads: was this a cameo appearance by Minneapolis legend Prince, at that time known by a symbol rather than his birth name? It was indeed Prince's symbol knocked onto its side, with a smiley face inside, but it turned out to be the Coens making a little mischief. The victim was actually played by crew member J. Todd Anderson. As Ethan explained, 'The storyboard artist formerly known as J. Todd Anderson decided he no longer wanted to go by that name'.

Anderson wasn't the only member of the *Fargo* crew to be executed on screen. The **Night Parking Attendant** at the Dayton-Radisson ramp, despatched by an irate and bleeding Carl Showalter, was played by Don 'Bix' Skahill, who was otherwise employed as the office production assistant on set ('I made coffee and copies'). In making copies of the script, he noticed the single-line role of the attendant and pressed the brothers into giving him the part.

The Coens weren't the only St Louis Park siblings to make a cultural impact nationally. In fact, they weren't the only residents of Flag Avenue South to do so. **The Hautmans**,

Norm Gunderson's wildlife-painting rivals, weren't a fictional creation. Contemporaries of Joel and Ethan, the three Hautman brothers are nationally renowned artists, celebrated in particular for their uber-realistic representations of Minnesota's wildfowl population. Indeed, it's their work that sits on the easels in Norm's bedroom studio. As kids, the Hautmans lived at number 1315, just eight doors up from the Coen homestead.

The name of the bar at which Mr Mohra works – **Ecklund & Swedlin's** – is a barely disguised reference to a name from the Coens' early years. Ecklund & Swedlund Homes was a construction company that, in the 1950s, began to develop the wide-open lands of St Louis Park. The Coen house on Flag Avenue South, along with most of the homes within a radius of a mile or two, was an Ecklund & Swedlund construction.

Finally, and it might just be a series of coincidences, but I'm positing the idea that, when picking the location in which to shoot Jerry's capture, the Coens selected that particular motel for a very specific reason. I've done a little digging and it turns out that the **Hitching Post Motel** sits on a stretch of Highway 61 that's also known as Trooper Glen Skalman Memorial Highway. It was here in 1964 that Trooper Skalman was fatally shot after pulling over a car, with the search for the suspect initially being based on the partial licence plate that the trooper had written in his notebook. Sound familiar? Plus, the suspect was eventually apprehended on Fremont Avenue in Minneapolis. The Coens chose Fremont Terrace in Minneapolis as Shep Proudfoot's address. As Marge says, 'It'd be quite a coincidence if they weren't, ya know, connected.'

I think she might agree a hunnert percent on my policework here.

EPILOGUE

Nearly twenty-five years after stumbling out of Canal Place Cinema in New Orleans, I'm yet again reading the 'THIS IS A TRUE STORY' notice. The DVD is back in the machine.

Reading the notice for the first time is my eldest son. I'm not one for imposing your tastes on your teenage offspring. Let them find their own things, their own cultural identity. But, y'know, *Fargo* is *Fargo*. He *needs* to see it. Everyone does. Think of it as a parental duty, one that serves up life lessons to carry with him into future decades. The next ninety-four minutes will teach him multiple things: that commissioning your significant other to be kidnapped is bad; that extorting money from a rich relative is bad; that shooting a state trooper is bad. And that getting your money's worth at an all-you-can-eat buffet makes strong economic sense.

Over the next hour and a half, he laughs in all the right places – the interview with the truck-stop hookers; the wide-eyed expression of the first parking attendant demanding his four dollars; Showalter's attempt at 'total fucking silence' – even if some of the nuances of the plot aren't crystal-clear to him from this first watch.

No matter. He'll return another time. For any and every first-time viewer, *Fargo* leaves plenty of uncertainties to straighten out and multiple ambiguities to ponder. I remember it took several viewings for it to dawn on me that Jean was dead on the kitchen floor of the cabin; I thought (hoped) she was merely unconscious. The vertical lines of blood streaking down the fridge were the eventual giveaway.

That's the beauty of *Fargo*. It's one of the Coens' most linear films, yet plenty remains blurred. Things don't necessarily get spelled out. Their films aren't always written in full sentences. Layers reveal themselves gradually, at leisure.

And *Fargo* is dense too, but in a good way. There's a lot packed in, making repeat viewings mandatory – and rewarding. Just now, on this latest showing, I spotted a few little details that have passed me by so many times. They're not integral to the plot, but they still enrich this umpteenth (and, by now, deeply forensic) viewing. For instance, never before had I spotted that, at the cabin, the oven grill is always on, always turned up high, to warm up Jean who, in her inadequate leisurewear, is positioned in front of it. It's a rare indication of empathy from the kidnappers.

Also, it had evaded me thus far that the Brainerd PD badge, specially designed for the film, features a silhouette of – who else? – Paul Bunyan and his sidekick ox. And is anyone else aware that, in the Lundegaards' en-suite bathroom, the magazine rack somewhat curiously contains a copy of *Playboy*?

Perhaps I've reached the point where I'm diving in too deep. But I love the fact that, after quarter of a century, I'm still discovering little morsels like these to snack on.

At the same time, though, I also never want to know every single last thing. Not everything must be revealed.

A lot can happen in the middle of nowhere, but some secrets should stay buried in the snow.

DRAMATIS PERSONAE

(in order of appearance)

Jerry Lundegaard	WILLIAM H MACY
Carl Showalter	STEVE BUSCEMI
Gaear Grimsrud	PETER STORMARE
Jean Lundegaard	KRISTIN RUDRÜD
Wade Gustafson	HARVE PRESNELL
Scotty Lundegaard	TONY DENMAN
Bucky the angry customer	GARY HOUSTON
Bucky's wife	SALLY WINGERT
Car salesman	KURT SCHWEICKHARDT
Hooker #1	LARISSA KOKERNOT
Hooker #2	MELISSA PETERMAN
Shep Proudfoot	STEVE REEVIS
Reilly Diefenbach	WARREN KEITH
Morning show co-host #1	STEVE EDELMAN
Morning show co-host #2	SHARON ANDERSON
Stan Grossman	LARRY BRANDENBURG
State trooper	JAMES GAULKE
Victim in field	J TODD ANDERSON

Victim in car	MICHELLE SUZANNE LE DOUX
Marge Gunderson	FRANCES McDORMAND
Norm Gunderson	JOHN CARROLL LYNCH
Lou	BRUCE BOHNE
Cashier	PETRA BODEN
Mike Yanagita	STEVE PARK
Customer	WAYNE EVENSON
Officer Olson	CLIFF RAKERD
Hotel clerk	JESSICA SHEPHERD
Airport parking lot attendant	PETER SCHMITZ
Mechanic	STEVE SHAEFER
Escort	MICHELLE HUTCHISON
Man in hallway	DAVID LOMAX
José Feliciano	JOSÉ FELICIANO
Night parking attendant	DON WILLIAM SKAHILL
Mr Mohra	BAIN BOEHLE
Valerie	ROSE STOCKTON
Bismarck police officer #1	ROBERT OZASKY
Bismarck police officer #2	JOHN BANDEMER
Directed by	JOEL COEN
Written by	ETHAN COEN AND JOEL COEN
Produced by	ETHAN COEN
Executive producers	TIM BEVAN
	ERIC FELLNER
Director of photography	ROGER DEAKINS, A.S.C.
Music by	CARTER BURWELL
Edited by	RODERICK JAYNES

ACKNOWLEDGEMENTS

Thanks . . .

. . . to everyone at Polaris, especially editor Peter Burns and copy-editor Alison Rae.

. . . to my *Fargo*-quoting agent, Kevin Pocklington at The North Literary Agency.

. . . Robin Askew, Jamie Bowman, Joe Cahill, Nigel Floyd and Paul Jacobs for particular favours and/or forensic clarification of various details.

. . . and to Jane, my companion at Canal Place Cinema twenty-five years ago and ever since.